D1490186

BLACKBEARD'S LAST FIGHT

Pirate Hunting in North Carolina 1718

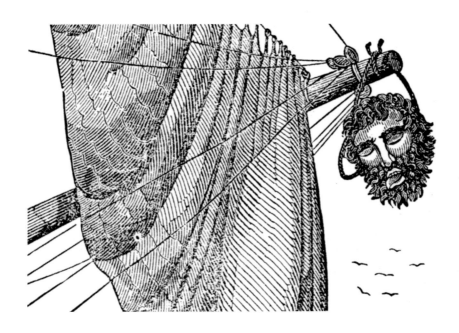

ANGUS KONSTAM

First published in Great Britain in 2013 by Osprey Publishing,
Midland House, West Way, Botley, Oxford, OX2 0PH, UK
43-01 21st Street, Suite 220B, Long Island City, NY 11101
E-mail: info@ospreypublishing.com

Osprey Publishing is part of the Osprey Group

A CIP catalogue record for this book is available from the British Library

Print ISBN: 978 1 78096 195 8
PDF ebook ISBN: 978 1 78096 196 5
ePub ebook ISBN: 978 1 78096 197 2

Index by Zoe Ross
Typeset in Sabon
Maps by bounford.com
3D BEV by Alan Gilliland
Originated by PDQ Media, Bungay, UK
Printed in China through Worldprint Ltd

13 14 15 16 17 10 9 8 7 6 5 4 3 2 1

Osprey Publishing is supporting the Woodland Trust, the UK's leading
woodland conservation charity, by funding the dedication of trees.

www.ospreypublishing.com

EDITOR'S NOTE

For ease of comparison please refer to the following conversion table:

1 nautical mile = 2,000 yards (1,800m)
1 mile = 1.6km
1yd = 0.9m
1ft = 0.3m
1in = 2.54cm/25.4mm
1 long ton = 1.016 metric tonnes
1lb = 0.45kg

ARTIST'S NOTE

Readers may care to note that the original paintings from which the
battlescenes of this book were prepared are available for private sale.
All reproduction copyright whatsoever is retained by the Publishers. All
enquiries should be addressed to:

mark@mrstacey.plus.com

The Publishers regret that they can enter into no correspondence upon
this matter.

All other illustrations are supplied courtesy of the Stratford Archive.

CONTENTS

INTRODUCTION

These days, pirates are generally regarded as larger-than-life caricatures – people who exist more in the pages of fiction or the cinema screen than in the historical past. Like gunfighters of the Wild West or Arthurian warriors they are usually seen as semi-fictional creatures, whose real exploits have been submerged in a tidal wave of myth and fictional make-believe. Despite the recent upsurge of piracy in East African waters, piracy has largely become divorced from the harsh realities which once surrounded it, or which still do today.

To the seafarers of the early 18th century piracy was no fantasy. It was a brutal and very real threat to their lives and livelihood. To sail through the pirate-infested waters of the American Atlantic seaboard or the Caribbean was to risk an encounter with pirates who bore no resemblance to our modern caricature of them. These people would kill indiscriminately, torture for amusement, and rob for their own gratification. If the seaman was lucky he would escape with his life. Others were not so fortunate.

Of course, piracy wasn't a new phenomenon. It had existed since ancient times – even Julius Caesar had an encounter with pirates some 1,800 years before Blackbeard was first heard of. Piracy was a cyclical curse – it thrived in areas where there was little central authority or effective naval presence, and it was generally suppressed through the imposition of law, and by aggressive naval patrolling. The decade from 1714 to 1724 saw one of these dramatic increases.

Pirates established themselves in the Bahamas, and ranged as far afield as Newfoundland and the coast of Brazil, attacking merchant ships, and largely evading capture. It took a concerted effort to quell this tide of crime, but by 1718 it looked as though it was largely under control. Only a few pirate crews remained at large. One of them was led by Edward Teach – better known as Blackbeard. He was only one of many pirates who operated in these waters during this period – an age known as 'The Golden Age of Piracy'. Others included Bartholomew Roberts ('Black Bart'), Charles Vane,

'Calico Jack' Rackam, 'Gentleman' Stede Bonnet, 'Black Sam' Bellamy, and the two women pirates Anne Bonny and Mary Read. Despite their exploits, most of these pirates are now half-forgotten. By contrast Blackbeard still remains a household name. Others were more brutal, or captured more ships, or had longer piratical careers. It was Blackbeard, however, who became the most notorious pirate of his day, and who remains so some three centuries after his death.

There are three main reasons for this. First of all, Blackbeard looked the part. He cultivated a sinister appearance to intimidate his victims, and this made him a larger-than-life character even while he was still alive. Secondly, his exploits formed the core of a biography of pirates, published just eight years after his death. He quickly became the archetypal pirate of the 'Golden Age'. Finally, in 1718 he almost single-handedly brought merchant trade to a halt in colonial North America. His blockade of Charleston caused such widespread alarm that he became the 18th-century equivalent of 'Public Enemy Number One'.

More than anything this attack against the main port of the South Carolina colony made Blackbeard the most feared pirate in American waters. The fragile economies of the American colonies relied extensively on maritime trade, and Blackbeard posed such a serious threat to this economic lifeline that action had to be taken. This, though, occurred at the time of a royal initiative to pardon pirates who turned themselves in, in the belief that this would reduce the scale of the problem. While the policy worked, it also meant that Blackbeard remained a threat, whether he was actively cruising for prey or not.

While most colonial governors limited their response to complaining to London and demanding naval protection, Governor Alexander Spotswood of Virginia was a man of action, who decided to take matters into his own hands. Even though Blackbeard was officially a pardoned criminal, and resident in a neighbouring colony, Spotswood decided to attack the pirate in his own lair, and so remove the threat he posed once and for all.

Therefore the scene was set for what would become the most successful anti-piracy raid of the entire 'Golden Age of Piracy'. What unfolded was a drama worthy of a Hollywood film, only one with a real piratical cast, and which actually happened. Just over 300 years ago, the most notorious pirate in history met his match.

According to his first biographer, Captain Johnson, Edward Teach was known as Blackbeard 'from the hair, which, like a frightful meteor, covered his whole face, and frightened America more than any comet that had appeared there a long time'.

ORIGINS

The making of Blackbeard

The story of Blackbeard really begins with a peace treaty, and a fleet of Spanish treasure ships. The signing of this treaty and the wrecking of the Spanish treasure fleet took place within two years of each other, and the two events conspired to produce a wave of crime that threatened to cripple the fragile economy of the American colonies. Today this wave of criminal activity is often referred to as 'The Golden Age of Piracy'. To the victims of pirates such as Blackbeard there was nothing 'golden' about it.

The signing of the Peace of Utrecht in April 1713 marked the end of the fighting between France, Spain, Great Britain, Portugal and Holland in the War of the Spanish Succession (1701–14). While the war between France and Austria dragged on for another year, the conflict between Europe's principal maritime powers was now over. For more than a decade the Caribbean basin had been a theatre of war, and privateers of all these nations had sailed its waters, preying on the merchant shipping of their nation's enemies. When news of the peace treaty reached the Americas that June, all these lucrative privateering contracts were rendered null and void. Thousands of well-armed seamen found themselves out of work, and many were unwilling to return to their previous mundane and poorly paid employment as merchant seamen. Privateering had given them a taste for plunder.

Effectively privateering was nothing more than state-sponsored piracy. When a war began a sea captain or ship owner could apply to his government for a letter of marque. The aspiring privateer agreed to attack the merchant shipping of his country's enemies, and to take the prizes into a friendly port where the ship and cargo would be sold. This was all perfectly legal in time of war. In return the government got a share of the proceeds – the level was usually set at 10 per cent. Obviously this was an extremely lucrative arrangement for everyone except the foreign ship owners, and of course foreign governments were doing exactly the same thing. It has been estimated that during the War of the Spanish Succession more than 300 privateers of various nationalities were operating in American waters, from Newfoundland down to Brazil. Most based themselves in the Caribbean, where the trade in rum, sugar and slaves ensured there was no shortage of prizes.

Profits were high – the owner of a 'private man-of-war' could recoup the cost of investment in just one short successful cruise. Privateering ships earned small fortunes for their owners and captains, but the crews were also well rewarded. Rather than receiving a regular wage like normal seamen they received a share of prize money – the money raised from selling the captured ship and its cargo. A successful privateering crewman could make more money in a single cruise than he could during a lifetime on board a merchant ship. It was little wonder that when the war ended many were tempted to continue plundering ships, regardless of the legality of their actions. While there might have been a peacetime boom in mercantile activity, many privateersmen were reluctant to return to the poor wages and harsh discipline of the merchant service.

For the British the centre of privateering activity in the Caribbean was Jamaica. Port Royal had been an infamous buccaneering base during the 17th century, when English, French and Dutch seamen used this roistering harbour while raiding the Spanish Main. Much of their plunder was spent in the port's taverns and brothels, at a time when Port Royal was being labelled 'The Sodom of the New World'. A combination of a devastating earthquake and tsunami in 1692 and a peace treaty in 1697 brought this roistering period to an end, but the harbour remained a useful haven for privateers a decade later when war returned to the Caribbean.

We don't know it for sure, but Blackbeard was almost certainly based there during the last years of the War of the Spanish Succession. The trouble with pirates in this period is that, like most seamen, very little is known about them until they crossed the line from law-abiding sailor to dangerous criminal. Blackbeard's real name was almost certainly Edward Teach, but he only appears in the historical record at the very start of the 'Golden Age of Piracy'. His first biographer, Captain Charles Johnson, writing in 1724, claimed that 'Edward Teach was a Bristol man born, but had sailed some time out of Jamaica in privateers, in the late French War'. He added that 'he had often distinguished himself for his uncommon boldness and personal courage', but that 'he was never raised to any command'.

By 1715 the mean streets of Port Royal were filled with seamen down on their luck, or men squandering the last of their privateering money before they left to seek gainful employment elsewhere. Then, appearing like manna from heaven, came the news of an epic disaster. For almost two centuries the Spanish had sent an annual fleet of treasure ships from the Caribbean to Spain. They carried a fortune in silver ingots, gold bars, silver and gold coins, plus emeralds and spices. The Spanish had come to rely on these ships arriving in Seville. Only three times – in 1554, 1622 and 1628 – had the fleet failed to reach Spain. In 1628 the fleet had been captured by the Dutch, and on the other two occasions it was struck by a hurricane and wrecked. That was exactly what happened in 1715. The treasure *flota* left Havana on

In this depiction of Blackbeard by Frank Schoonover, the pirate captain has tied his beard 'with ribbons, in small tails' as described by Captain Johnson. While many depictions of Blackbeard are largely fanciful, all draw on Johnson's description for their inspiration.

24 July, and a week later it was threading its way through the Bahamas Channel, between Florida and the Bahamian archipelago. On the evening of 30 July the ships were hit by a fearsome hurricane, which dashed the fleet against the reefs and sandbars of the Florida coast. Only one ship survived, and she limped back to Havana with the news.

A rescue expedition was duly sent out, not to rescue any survivors but to salvage what they could of the lost treasure. Unfortunately for the Spanish, news of the disaster had also reached Jamaica. In November 1715 Governor Hamilton of Jamaica sent two sloops on an anti-piracy patrol, under the command of Captain Henry Jennings, a former privateer. Unbeknown to the governor, Jennings rendezvoused with three other sloops crammed with ex-privateers, and then set off in search of Spanish treasure. We are reasonably sure that Edward Teach took part in this venture and was on board one of the five Jamaican sloops.

Jennings and his 300 adventurers landed close to the wrecked ships, and attacked the salvage camp, driving off the 60 Spanish guards. They then helped themselves to the treasure, and returned to Jamaica with their sloops filled with 60,000 pieces-of-eight. Back in Jamaica Governor Hamilton wisely turned a blind eye to the celebrations that ensued. By then treasure fever had swept the Caribbean, and hundreds of former privateers and other sailors joined Jennings' men. The Spanish were furious, and sent troops to protect their salvors. They also lodged a formal complaint with Governor Hamilton, who was forced to intercede. Before the troops arrived Jennings struck again, and this time he doubled his haul. That was the last of the plunder – the Spanish sent two large warships to carry home what remaining treasure they could find.

APRIL 1713

Peace of Utrecht – Britain and France make peace; privateering contracts now invalid

New Providence is the small island to the left of the phrase *Tropique du Cancer* in this detail from an early 18th-century French map of the Atlantic seaboard of North America. Ocracoke is below *Cap Hatteras*, to the left of the word *MER*.

30 JULY 1715

Wrecking of the Spanish treasure *flota*

While this engraving shows the pirate George Lowther, in the background a group of pirates can be seen, wearing the clothing worn by most seamen of this period. The wearing of sashes and headscarves is an inaccurate, modern addition to early 18th-century pirate dress.

By then – the spring of 1716 – Jennings was *persona non grata* in Jamaica, as he had disobeyed the governor's explicit orders. He needed a new base. He settled on the island of New Providence in the Bahamas, a place that lay beyond the reach of the authorities, and which had already become a minor haven for former privateers turned pirate. The arrival of Jennings turned this small pirate haven into a boom town. The pirates who had already based themselves there were led by Benjamin Hornigold, a former privateer who was now a pirate with scruples. He tried to avoid attacking British ships and generally adhered to the terms of his old privateering 'letter of marque'. The French and the Spanish, though, were fair game. He had about 200 men under his command, and they operated in the nearby Bahamas Channel, between the Bahamas and Florida.

Jennings and his men soon turned to piracy, and many joined Hornigold's crew. By the summer of 1716 New Providence was a hive of illegal activity, with treasure hunters using the islands to raid the wreck sites, while others made a living through piracy. The result was a marked increase in the number of piratical attacks, both in the Bahamas Channel and in the Florida Strait. Soon these Bahamian pirates were ranging as far afield as the seaboard of

Britain's American colonies, and the islands of the West Indies. On 3 June Governor Spotswood of the Virginia colony wrote to the Council of Trade in London, complaining about this upsurge in piracy. He added that pirates had taken over the Bahamas.

By early 1717 it was reported that there were over 500 pirates in New Providence, and at least a dozen small pirate vessels, mainly sloops and brigantines. Makeshift taverns and brothels were established there, and merchants from Jamaica and the West Indies visited the islands to buy the pirate plunder at knock-down prices. Most merchant ships of the time carried mundane cargoes such as tobacco, rum, cotton, sugar or timber. If the cargoes couldn't be consumed by the pirates themselves they were worthless, unless they could find merchants unscrupulous enough to buy stolen goods. This is exactly what happened in New Providence.

So, what of Blackbeard – Edward Teach? His biographer Captain Johnson reported that 'He went a-pirating, which I think was in the latter end of the year 1716, when Captain Benjamin Hornigold put him in a sloop that he had made prize of, and with whom he continued in consortship till a little while before Hornigold surrendered'. In other words, Blackbeard started his piratical career as one of Hornigold's crew, based in New Providence during late 1716. It also seems clear that after Hornigold realized the potential of his recruit, he became Blackbeard's mentor, and eventually gave him command of one of his prizes.

Then in March 1717 we have an official confirmation of Blackbeard's new status. Captain Munthe of South Carolina ran his sloop aground on the western fringe of the Bahamas, and while he was freeing his vessel he questioned local fishermen about pirate activity in the area. They told him that five main pirate captains were operating from New Providence, including Hornigold, Jennings and 'Thatch'. The latter, who commanded a six-gun sloop and 70 men, could only be Edward Teach. He was still sailing in consort with Hornigold, and that spring their two sloops cruised off the Atlantic seaboard, capturing several prizes, and generally making a nuisance of themselves.

What ended this association with Benjamin Hornigold was a royal pardon. The British Government had offered to pardon any pirates who willingly gave themselves up. Hornigold, who always claimed he was a privateer, not a pirate, decided to accept the offer. His crew rebelled at this, and Hornigold was deposed as captain. It was probably at this point that Blackbeard decided to forge his own path. Certainly by September he was cruising independently, as a pirate captain in his own right. On 29 September 1717 he attacked the sloop *Betty* of Virginia, which was returning home with her hold laden with wine. The pirates drank their fill, and then sank their prize, leaving the crew a boat in which to row ashore.

So began the cruise of Captain Edward Teach, who lacked Hornigold's scruples when it came to British or colonial American prizes. What followed was a voyage that would make Blackbeard's piratical name, and would threaten to bring the maritime trade of Britain's North American colonies to a standstill. The legend of Blackbeard was about to begin.

This anchor was recovered from the wreck of Blackbeard's *Queen Anne's Revenge*, which foundered in Topsail Inlet (now Beaufort Inlet), near the modern port of Beaufort, NC. The site has produced a wealth of artefacts, most of which are now on display in the North Carolina Maritime Museum.

29 SEPTEMBER 1717

Teach's first independent attack

Blackbeard's cruise

In late September 1717 Blackbeard was off the Virginia Capes, where he captured the sloop *Betty*. With hindsight he would have been better cruising off a colony where the governor was less enthusiastic in waging a war against piracy. All Blackbeard achieved there was to get his crew drunk, and annoy Governor Spotswood of Virginia. We don't know the name of Blackbeard's pirate sloop, but in early November the *Boston News Letter* printed a report from a Captain Codd, who had been sailing from Dublin to Philadelphia when he was attacked, 'by a pirate sloop called *Revenge* of 12 guns, 150 men, commanded by one Teach.'

Blackbeard was clearly coming up in the world – during the summer he had doubled the size of his crew, and the number of guns he carried. He let Codd's ship go, largely because she was carrying indentured servants. Many of these might well have joined Blackbeard's crew – his crew increased largely thanks to volunteers recruited from captured merchantmen. The same newspaper mentioned five other pirate attacks which took place off the coast of Delaware in mid-October, and although Teach wasn't named we can be fairly certain that he was responsible. In one of them the pirates kept their prize, the sloop *Sea Nymph* from Bristol, outward bound from Philadelphia to Oporto. Every time he captured a ship, Blackbeard recruited new crewmen from it. Now he had a second ship for these new recruits to crew.

The *Sea Nymph* didn't last long – a week later Blackbeard captured a 'great sloop' bound from Curaçao with a cargo of cocoa. The beans were thrown overboard, but the pirates kept this new vessel, and gave the *Sea Nymph* to Captain Goulet and his men, who sailed on to Philadelphia. This example of 'trading up' was a typical ploy of pirates of the period. Soon Blackbeard would do it again, but in a much more spectacular fashion. Before the *Sea Nymph* was over the horizon the pirates had captured three more ships. It was suggested in the newspaper that Blackbeard's force consisted of more than one sloop. This fits in with the tally of his prizes. However, the mention of his ship name – the *Revenge* – shows that Blackbeard didn't confine his attacks to merchant ships.

In the *Boston News Letter* article about Captain Codd's encounter with Teach, it mentioned that 'On board the Pirate Sloop is Major Bennet, but has no command; He walks about in his morning gown, and then to his books, of which he has a good library on board'. This was a misprint for Major Stede Bonnet of the Barbados militia. A few months earlier he decided to abandon his wife and plantation, and to become a pirate. He actually bought a sloop – the *Revenge* – and hired a crew. Real pirates captured their ships – they didn't buy them. Somewhere off Virginia or Delaware Bonnet fell in with Blackbeard, who decided to take the major under his protection. Effectively this meant Blackbeard commandeered his sloop and his crew, and Bonnet became a virtual prisoner on board his own vessel.

By the end of October Blackbeard was off New Jersey. Winter was approaching, and like many pirates Blackbeard favoured a pattern of cruising off the Atlantic seaboard in summer and then heading south into the warmer waters of the Caribbean for winter. The hurricane season lasts from June to November, which was another reason pirates often avoided the Caribbean during this period. Consequently Blackbeard decided to set a course towards the south, passing down the eastern side of the Bahamas to reach the Leeward Islands. At this point it seems that Blackbeard had two sloops under his command – the *Revenge* and the 'great sloop'. It seems Blackbeard's original sloop – the one given to him by Hornigold – had returned to New Providence.

His two remaining vessels reached the Caribbean in early November, and by the 17th they were some 60 miles off Martinique. A lookout spotted a ship on the horizon, and Blackbeard gave chase. She was eventually overhauled and surrendered after a token fight. She turned out to be the French slave ship *La Concorde* of 200 tons, bound from Nantes to Martinique.

He took his prize to a secluded anchorage off the nearby island of Bequia, and there he set about converting *La Concorde* into the ultimate pirate ship. The slave ship carried 16 guns, but Blackbeard carried spare guns in the holds of his two sloops – ordnance taken from prizes. His men cut extra gun ports in the slave ship, and got rid of her forecastle and quarterdeck, to create a more efficient fighting platform. By the time they finished, the new pirate flagship carried no fewer than 40 guns, which made her more than a match for any merchantman she encountered, and more powerful than most of the warships in American waters. Blackbeard named his new flagship *Queen Anne's Revenge*.

17 NOVEMBER 1717

Teach captures *La Concorde* – renames her *Queen Anne's Revenge*

This early 18th-century engraving of a French merchant ship depicts a three-masted vessel of a similar size and appearance as *La Concorde*, the slave ship from Nantes which Blackbeard captured, and then converted into the *Queen Anne's Revenge*.

Leaving the slaves on Bequia, Blackbeard began his cruise through the Leeward Islands, and captured his first prize a week later. Next was a merchant ship from Boston – the *Great Allen* – which was plundered then burned. Four more sloops followed, all captured between St Vincent and Anguilla. The last of these was the *Margaret*, commanded by a Captain Bostock. In his report of the attack Bostock claimed that the pirates attacked him with a large ship and a sloop, and that the flagship was crewed by 300 men 'with much gold dust aboard'. Then he described the pirate captain, who he called 'Captain Tach'. This pirate was 'a tall spare man with a very black beard which he wore very long'. As a result, this pirate captain with his powerful ship was about to earn a nickname that would strike terror throughout the Americas. Blackbeard had come of age.

During these attacks Teach learned that a powerful British warship was out looking for him – the 30-gun *Scarborough*. While Blackbeard's *Queen Anne's Revenge* had more guns, her crew was largely untrained in gunnery, and they would have little chance in a straight fight with a powerful British frigate. His biographer Captain Johnson has Blackbeard fighting the *Scarborough*, but this is pure invention. The two ships never met. Sensibly Blackbeard decided to quit the Leeward Islands before he was cornered by the *Scarborough*, and he headed towards Hispaniola, where he sought refuge in Samana Bay. There he probably careened his ships – weeds and barnacles were scraped off the hulls – to make them sail faster. The pirates no doubt also celebrated Christmas by eating, drinking and enjoying themselves.

In February Blackbeard set off westwards towards the Gulf of Honduras, and the coast of Central America. This was usually a busy place, as ships regularly anchored in the bay to collect cargoes of logwood. Blackbeard probably avoided Jamaica, where the Royal Navy maintained a guard ship, and by late March he reached what is now Belize. Off the Turneffe Islands he captured a Jamaican sloop called the *Adventure*, and kept the fast 80-ton vessel for himself. Therefore Blackbeard commanded three craft by the time he reached the logwood anchorages. The three vessels fanned out to cover a larger area, and four rich prizes were caught in their net – a three-masted sailing ship called three-masted sailing ship the *Protestant Caesar*, and three more sloops. All these prizes were plundered and burned.

By the end of April Blackbeard was ready to sail north again. He wanted to leave the Caribbean before the start of the hurricane season, and so he headed north through the Yucatan Channel, and then rounded the western tip of Cuba. He sailed along Cuba's northern coast to reach the Florida Straits, and off Havana he captured a small Spanish sloop. He kept her,

The 'gentleman pirate', Major Stede Bonnet, was a plantation owner and militia officer from Barbados who gave up his prosperous but dull life to become a pirate. After effectively being held prisoner by Blackbeard, Bonnet was abandoned by him at Topsail Inlet.

which meant that as his force entered the familiar waters of the Bahamas Channel Blackbeard had three sloops under his command, as well as his 40-gun flagship. With such a powerful squadron at his disposal Blackbeard must have felt invincible.

This was probably why he felt confident enough to undertake his most ambitious attack yet. On 22 May 1718 the pirate flotilla appeared off Charles Town (now Charleston), in the South Carolina colony. A long sandbar separated Charles Town Harbour from the sea, and there was only one gap in it deep enough to allow large ships to pass. Even then the ships usually needed the help of a pilot. Blackbeard positioned his pirate squadron just outside this channel, and effectively placed the port under blockade.

The pirates' first victim was the pilot boat that came out to help the new arrivals past the Charles Town bar. She was accompanied by the *Crowley*, a large merchantman bound for London. Soon both vessels were in the hands of the pirates. Two more outward-bound ships were captured the following day, one of them the *William*, a large British merchantman. After that the authorities realized what was happening, and the remaining ships in Charles Town remained trapped in the harbour. This was an incredible act for a pirate. Until now, pirates had preyed on individual ships on the high seas. Not since the days of the 17th century buccaneers had anything so audacious been attempted. Now Blackbeard was holding a whole port to ransom, one of the richest in Britain's North American colonies.

That, of course, was his intention. He planned to make whatever money he could from the situation, and then disappear before the Royal Navy could send warships to break the blockade. The nearest Royal Navy squadron was in Virginia's James River. It would take a week to contact them, and another week for the warships to reach Charles Town. In the meantime the pirates were in control. Captain Johnson described the effect this was having on the city's inhabitants. The blockade 'struck a great terror to the whole province of Carolina … that they abandoned themselves to despair, being in no condition to resist their force'. Trade was completely disrupted – until Blackbeard left, no ship could get in or out. The city fathers awaited the pirates' demands.

When they came they were surprisingly lenient. Blackbeard sent some of his captives ashore with a demand for a chest of medicine. The pirates who escorted them added that if this simple demand wasn't met then their companions 'would murder their prisoners, send up their heads to the governor, and set the ships they had taken on fire'. While the governor of the South Carolina colony sent for help, he and his advisors considered their options. The port was defended by artillery batteries and local militia, but their effectiveness was questionable. The easiest thing was to agree to Blackbeard's demands. So a medicine chest valued at £300–£400 was sent aboard the *Queen Anne's Revenge*, and for the moment the pirates seemed satisfied.

In fact Blackbeard had already looted a small fortune – around £1,500 – from the passengers of the *Crowley*, as well as money and supplies from the other ships. To demand a ransom from the city would involve lengthy negotiation, and Blackbeard knew that time was not on his side. The importance of the medicine has never been fully explained, but the most likely reason is that the pirate captain and his crew might have contracted a disease; either a venereal one from their winter stay in Hispaniola, or else the flux – yellow fever – from their time in the Gulf of Honduras. Whatever the reason, Blackbeard seemed pleased with his ransom and his ships raised their blockade, and sailed away over the horizon.

Blackbeard knew that this daring assault would raise a whirlwind of indignation, and he would be branded the most notorious criminal in the Americas. He needed somewhere to lie low for a while, where he could divide his plunder and plan his next move. He must have considered his options. He could sail off to the north, to prey on the untouched waters

Charles Town (now Charleston, SC) lay at the far end of a wide natural harbour, which was separated from the sea by a long sandbar. By blocking the only navigable channel through it, Blackbeard managed to blockade the port, one of the most prosperous in Britain's American colonies.

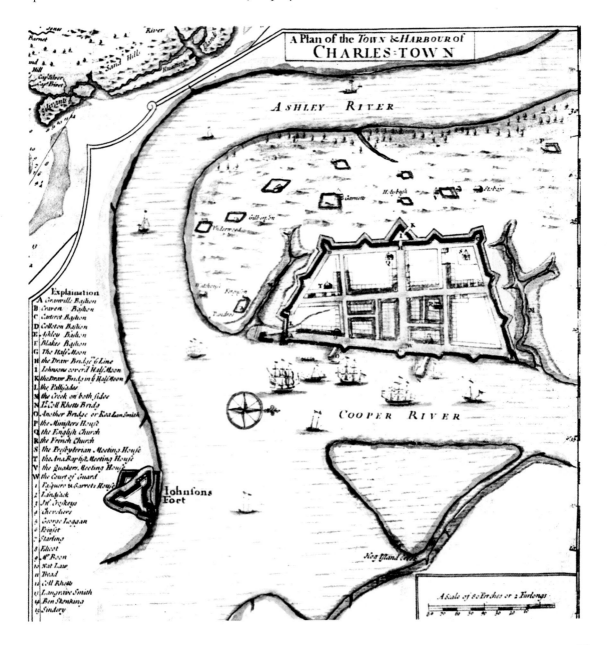

of New England, or he could cross the Atlantic to cruise the slaving grounds of West Africa. Both of these options entailed a fair degree of risk. Instead, Blackbeard began formulating another scheme – one that would give him a chance to treble his profit, and would give him immunity from the authorities. After his greatest triumph, Blackbeard was going to give up his piratical ways.

The pardon offered to pirates was still on offer, but Blackbeard had to be careful where he went to accept it. After all, his actions off Charles Town meant that technically he was ineligible, as he was still an active pirate. Since he left the Bahamas Hornigold and others had accepted a pardon, and were actively supporting the establishment of British rule there. That ruled out a return to his old base. Governor Spotswood of Virginia and Governor Hunter of New York were vehement in their opposition to what they saw as 'diehard' pirates such as Teach. Clearly, Blackbeard couldn't return to South Carolina either, as the governor there wasn't going to forgive the blockade of his main port. That left the colony of North Carolina. The problem was that the North Carolina colony was one of the least developed places on the Atlantic seaboard. Its one port – Bath Town – sat on an inland sound, protected from the sea by a line of islands and shifting sandbars. It would be the ideal place to establish a new base, while pretending to turn his back on piracy, but first Blackbeard had to get rid of the *Queen Anne's Revenge*. It was too large to pass through North Carolina's Outer Banks, and while it remained afloat it represented a direct threat to the Royal Navy.

Blackbeard came up with a novel solution. After leaving Charles Town he sailed north past the mouth of the Cape Fear River, and by the start of June he was approaching Cape Lookout, which marked the southern tip of the Outer Banks. Moving closer inshore he reached Topsail Inlet (now Beaufort Inlet), near the modern port of Beaufort, North Carolina. There was no town there in 1718 – only a handful of huts belonging to seasonal fishermen. The channel leading to the anchorage beyond the inlet was narrow – just 300 yards wide. Undeterred, Blackbeard sailed his flagship into the channel, with his sloops following on behind.

All of a sudden the *Queen Anne's Revenge* ran hard aground. Blackbeard called out to Israel Hands in the sloop *Adventure*, and asked him to tow the larger ship off the sandbar. Instead the *Adventure* ran aground too. It soon became clear that there was nothing to be done – the *Queen Anne's Revenge* was stuck fast, and was as good as lost. It is virtually certain that this is exactly what Blackbeard had intended. It was all part of his plan for 'downsizing' his piratical operation. Next, Blackbeard sent Major Bonnet off to Bath Town in the small Spanish sloop, to meet the colony's governor, and to arrange a provisional pardon.

As soon as Bonnet had sailed off, Blackbeard moved the plunder from his flagship to a small captured sloop. Next he landed most of his crew on the beach at Beaufort, and marooned those who remained loyal to Bonnet on a small island. This done, he stripped the *Revenge* of anything useful, and sailed off to the north. When Bonnet returned a week or so later he discovered that Blackbeard had abandoned over 200 of his men, and absconded with all the plunder. It was a dastardly move, even for a notorious pirate. Worse, Bonnet had also paved the way for Blackbeard to give himself up to the authorities. The major turned pirate was left penniless, and surrounded by pirates baying for revenge. After a few weeks of fruitless pursuit Bonnet eventually succumbed to the wishes of these men, and turned pirate again. Meanwhile Blackbeard was well on his way to becoming a pardoned man.

Blackbeard made his way to Bath Town, and in mid-June he accepted the King's Pardon from Governor Charles Eden of North Carolina. Officially, he and his 30 remaining men had turned their back on piracy. Unofficially he had already split the plunder with them, and they all realized that they were merely biding their time, waiting for the right time to resume their criminal career. Meanwhile the two taverns in the port would benefit from these boisterous and wealthy new customers, and their notorious captain became a source of curiosity in the colony, as he entertained the wealthier colonists with tales of his misdeeds. Others were less convinced that Blackbeard had indeed turned his back on his criminal past. In particular Governor Spotswood in neighbouring Virginia was sure that Blackbeard was up to no good. As soon as he had evidence, he would act, and rid the world of this dangerous character once and for all.

Numerous historical markers in North Carolina help identify the key locations in the Blackbeard story. This one is on Cedar Island, NC, near where passengers now board the ferry crossing Pamlico Sound to Ocracoke Island.

THE PLAN

Countering the pirate threat

Ironically, the reason Edward Teach was able to gain a pardon for his crimes was due to an anti-piracy policy adopted by the British Government. Faced with a dramatic upsurge in the incidence of piracy, the government considered its options. The Royal Navy had already been reduced in size after the end of the War of the Spanish Succession, and the Admiralty's budget had been cut. This meant it was unlikely that the navy could significantly increase its presence in American waters – at least not immediately. The other option was to reduce the number of active pirates in the Americas by offering a pardon to those willing to renounce their criminal ways.

This policy wasn't new. The government of King William III had introduced the scheme during the few brief years of peace after the last war with France, between 1697 and 1701. It worked then, and allowed the Royal Navy (working together with the Dutch) to concentrate their resources on the pirates who remained at large. Essentially it was a scheme designed to reduce the number of active pirates on the high seas. It certainly wasn't designed to reward those who accepted the pardon by letting them abscond with their plunder, but for the pirates that was the real attraction.

This was why Blackbeard's pirate mentor Benjamin Hornigold was so keen to accept the latest version of the pardon when it was issued in September 1717. He and Henry Jennings had made a small fortune through piracy and illegal treasure hunting, and when word of the royal proclamation reached the Caribbean that December they both saw a way of keeping their money without running the risk of capture and execution. Word of this scheme had already been discussed in the British and colonial American newspapers, so the proclamation came as no surprise to Hornigold and the others. What they didn't know until they read the details of it for themselves were the terms attached to it.

The document itself was impressively titled a 'Proclamation for Supressing Pyrates', and it stated that since 24 June 1715 the New Providence pirates had 'committed diverse piracies and robberies on the high seas, in the West Indies, or adjoining to our plantations'. The date was important – it was when the Spanish treasure fleet set sail from Havana. The implication is that the authorities in London recognized Jennings' attack on the salvage camp as marking the start of this recent pirate scourge. Then came the terms:

Alexander Spotswood (c. 1676–1740), the acting governor of the Virginia colony, was the man behind the attack on Blackbeard. Essentially he realized that if Governor Eden of North Carolina was unwilling to deal with the pirate, then he would have to intervene.

We have thought fit ... to issue this, our Royal Proclamation, and we do hereby promise and declare that in case any of the said pirates shall, on or before the 5th September in the year of our Lord 1718, surrender him or themselves to one of our principal Secretaries of State in Great Britain or Ireland, or to any Governor or Deputy Governor of any of our plantations beyond the seas; Every such pyrate or pyrates so surrendering him, or themselves, aforesaid, shall have our gracious pardon, of and for such, his or their piracy or piracies, by him or them committed before the 5th of January next ensuing.

Effectively this meant that Hornigold or any other pirate who applied for a pardon to a British colonial governor would be granted one, on two conditions. First, they had to apply within a year of the promulgation of the royal proclamation – by 5 September 1718. Secondly, any piratical attack carried out after 5 January 1718 wouldn't be forgiven, and the perpetrator would be ineligible for a pardon. Strangely, it seemed to give the pirates four months of grace, when they could attack at will, and still be pardoned afterwards. One would have thought this gave the pirates *carte blanche* to plunder freely, but in fact copies

The arrival of Governor Woodes Rogers in New Providence marked the end of piracy in the Bahamas. As a former privateer he understood how to deal with these privateers turned pirates, and enlisted the help of Benjamin Hornigold to help keep them in line.

of the proclamation only reached Jamaica in early December 1717, and it was the end of the month before Jamaican traders brought them to New Providence. That meant the pirates had no time to enjoy a last swansong if they wanted to receive the king's pardon.

This scheme was only part of the story. In effect it was the carrot. The proclamation also contained a very big stick. It continued: 'We do hereby strictly command and charge all our Admirals, Captains and other officers at sea and all our Governors and commanders ... to seize and take such of the pyrates, who shall refuse or neglect to surrender themselves accordingly'. It went on: 'We do hereby further declare, that in case any person or persons, on, or after the said pyrates ... shall have and receive a reward'.

This reward – a bounty on the head of any captured pirates – was set at £100 for a captain, £40 for a quartermaster, master or gunner, and £20 for any other pirates in the crew. This reward was earned for 'causing or

The pirate Charles Vane was the leader of the 'diehards' from the Bahamas who refused to accept Governor Rogers' pardon. He and his men spent a week or so in Blackbeard's company on Ocracoke in September 1718. He was eventually caught, and was executed in 1721.

procuring discovery or seizure'. If one of the pirate crew turned informer, and handed their own captain over to the authorities, then the reward was doubled – they could earn a pardon, and a reward of £200. In 1718 that was the equivalent of £40,000 (US $60,000) today.

While it wasn't actually said in the proclamation, the stick wasn't just a matter of offering blood money. It was matched by a policy of encouraging colonial governors and naval captains to be proactive, and to hunt down those pirates who refused to apply for a pardon. With fewer pirates to deal with the Royal Navy could therefore concentrate its limited resources on the ones who remained at large. By finding and capturing them they would then send a message to other would-be pirates, or to those who might consider reverting to their old ways. It had to be shown that piracy was not a sensible career option.

This was why hunting the pirates wasn't necessarily the end of it. Ideally many of the pirates would be captured rather than killed, which then raised the possibility of a public trial – where the outcome was rarely in any doubt – and a very public execution. Even this wasn't the end of it. After the public hanging the bodies of pirates were often liberally coated in pitch or tar to preserve the corpse, and then stuck inside iron cages, which were hung on gallows at the entrance of the harbour where the trial and execution took place. This was another very visible way of reinforcing the message that piracy didn't pay.

When news of this proclamation reached New Providence in December 1717 it divided the pirate community. It has been estimated that there were around 800 pirates based there at the time – a significant increase since the start of the year. For the same period the total number of pirates operating in American waters was probably double that – historians have placed the number at somewhere between 1,500 and 2,000. In other words, if the authorities could deal with the pirates in the Bahamas, then they would eradicate half of the pirate problem.

Benjamin Hornigold and Henry Jennings both planned to accept the pardon, but for two different reasons. Hornigold had been deposed by his crew, who rebelled against his limiting attacks to French and Spanish ships. For him the notion that he was still acting as a privateer was important, and set him apart from other pirates. The pardon offered a way for him to recover some of his lost dignity, and to regain his standing in New Providence. For Jennings the motive was more mercenary – he saw a way to retire with his plunder intact. Both men felt that the British authorities would be more willing to accept their contrition if they also encouraged their fellow pirates to follow their example. Captain Johnson recorded how they set about convincing their fellow pirates:

> They sent for those who went out a-cruising, and called a general council, but there was so much noise and clamour that nothing could be agreed on. Some were for fortifying the island, to stand upon their own terms, and treating with the government on the foot of [as] a commonwealth. Others were also for strengthening the island for their own security, but were not strenuous for these punctilios, so that

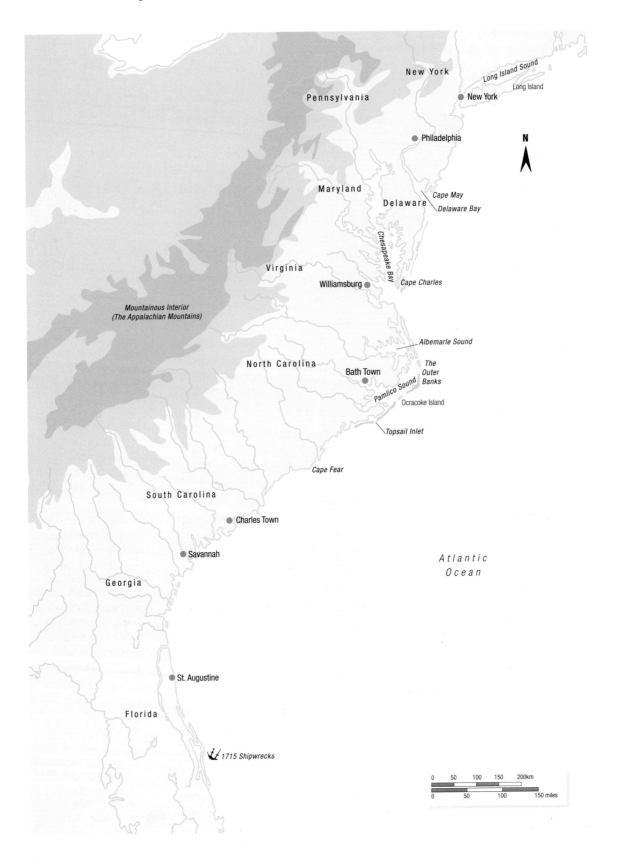

New York

Long Island Sound

Long Island

Pennsylvania

New York

Philadelphia

N

Maryland

Cape May

Delaware

Delaware Bay

Chesapeake Bay

Virginia

Williamsburg

Cape Charles

Mountainous Interior
(The Appalachian Mountains)

Albemarle Sound

North Carolina

The
Outer
Banks

Bath Town

Pamlico Sound

Ocracoke Island

Topsail Inlet

Cape Fear

South Carolina

Charles Town

Savannah

Atlantic
Ocean

Georgia

St. Augustine

Florida

1715 Shipwrecks

0   50   100   150   200km

0   50   100   150 miles

they might have a general pardon without being obliged to make any restitution, and to retire with all their effects to the neighbouring British plantations.

Hornigold and Jennings pointed out that the notion of forming a pirate 'commonwealth' to oppose the might of the British authorities was completely impractical. The British could easily bring overwhelming force to bear to destroy the pirate den. Many were swayed by the idea of being able to walk away – there was no mention in the royal proclamation of paying restitution to the victims of piracy. Eventually the two leaders managed to convince around 150 pirates to surrender to the authorities when the opportunity presented itself. Others – the diehard pirates led by Charles Vane – remained adamant. They wanted no pardon, and would continue their piratical careers regardless of the decision of their fellows.

That council probably took place in February 1718. The following month the frigate HMS *Phoenix* arrived, and Captain Pearce went ashore under flag of truce to see whether the pirates were likely to accept the pardon or not. He confirmed there was no requirement to pay restitution, and was delighted that so many of the pirates were willing to 'go straight'. After confirming there was no need for paying restitution a total of 209 pirates formally surrendered, and were issued with provisional pardons. While half of the pirates were still vacillating, Vane and his hardliners were becoming increasingly isolated.

Before he left in early April, Pearce told the assembled pirates that a British governor had been appointed, and would be arriving in a few months, backed up by a squadron of Royal Navy warships. While Vane and his supporters continued to attack ships, the rest of the New Providence pirates meekly awaited the arrival of British rule. In late July the new Bahamian governor, Woodes Rogers, duly arrived off New Providence, and was welcomed by the majority of the pirate community there. The exception was Charles Vane, who sailed a fire-ship in among the assembled British squadron, and made good his escape in the confusion, his sloop *Ranger* firing broadsides off to both sides as she went. While this was a spectacular exit it did little to alter the fact that New Providence was now closed to pirates. The Bahamas were now part of Britain's overseas dominions.

Although no portrait of Captain Brand survives, this depiction of a pirate-hunting contemporary, Captain Ogle, shows the uniform worn by a Royal Naval post captain during this period. It was Ogle who hunted down and killed the pirate Bartholomew 'Black Bart' Roberts.

Opposite: The Atlantic Seaboard of Colonial North America, as it appeared in 1718.

When Captain Pearce's *Phoenix* had left New Providence over three months earlier, Blackbeard was busy wreaking havoc among the logwood ships in the Gulf of Honduras. Like Vane he seemed to care little for the royal offer, and by late May his disregard for the scheme was demonstrated when he blockaded Charles Town. As all of these attacks had been carried out after the 5 January deadline given in the royal proclamation, Blackbeard was no longer eligible for a pardon. Instead he would be one of those diehard pirates who would be hunted down and made an example of. Amazingly, through luck or more probably forethought, the pirate approached the one colonial official who might be willing to overlook these recent crimes.

Blackbeard had captured enough British ships to learn all about the proclamation, and no doubt knew of the situation in the Bahamas. He realized New Providence was no longer open to him as a pirate base. Without one he would be unable to sell his plunder. Pirates needed shady merchants in order to prosper. The only solution seemed to be to surrender to the authorities, and to throw himself on the mercy of the governor of the North Carolina colony.

Blackbeard had targeted North Carolina for three good reasons. First, unlike neighbouring Virginia and South Carolina, the colony had no deep-water mercantile port, and so was less reliant on maritime trade. This meant the governor was less likely to be swayed by the influential merchants eager to seek justice against a notorious pirate. Second, the colony's only port was a struggling backwater, and its traders were more likely to provide the pirates with the shadowy trading deals they wanted. Finally, the governor was widely regarded as a soft touch.

Governor Charles Eden had been appointed by Queen Anne in May 1713, and had set up residence near Bath Town. He was almost 45 in the summer of 1718, and had prospered during his five years in office. His 400-acre plantation lay on the opposite bank of Bath Creek from the small town, while he had another at Sandy Point in Chowan County, several miles to the north, close to the modern town of Edenton. He and Edward Teach first met in late June 1718. The governor had already met Stede Bonnet at Sandy Point, and now he travelled south to Bath Town to meet the pirate. He must have been apprehensive, as Bonnet had told him Blackbeard's crew numbered over 300 men. He would surely have been mightily relieved when Blackbeard arrived with just two dozen pirates at his back.

The formalities were speedily dealt with. Blackbeard's activities off Charles Town were conveniently ignored, and Eden's deputy Tobias Knight dealt with all the paperwork. It may have been purely coincidental that Knight bought a substantial local estate around the time Blackbeard arrived in Bath Town, but after Governor Spotswood's intervention allegations were made that Knight was in collusion with Teach. Certainly there was plenty of circumstantial evidence pointing to a profitable business arrangement between the pirate and the colonial official but nothing was proved.

For Governor Eden the surrender of Blackbeard and his men must have seemed like a real political coup. After all, he had rid the colonies of the most notorious pirate in American waters. He seemed completely penitent, and earnest in his desire to give up his piratical ways. Teach and his men were duly pardoned, and having turned their backs on piracy they swore to become honest merchants, working for the common good of the colony. Teach even set himself up in a house near Bath Town, and showed every appearance of honouring his word. That summer Eden must have been delighted.

In nearby Virginia Governor Spotswood was less enthusiastic. Like his fellow British administrator Governor Robert Johnson of the South Carolina colony, Spotswood saw the pardon as a sham. Blackbeard had flouted the terms imposed by the king by blockading Charles Town. Now it seemed as if he would get away with it. Spotswood was determined to hold Teach to account for his actions, but he had no authority in North Carolina, and so he had to bide his time, hoping that Blackbeard would make a wrong move. Sure enough, this was exactly what happened.

During July Teach began taking his sloop *Adventure* away on 'fishing trips' in Pamlico Sound, and during this time he used the western side of Ocracoke Island as an anchorage. Ocracoke was one of the string of barrier islands that formed the Outer Banks, lying between Pamlico Sound and the Atlantic Ocean. These waters were shallow and contained numerous sandbars, which seemed to move with every hurricane or winter storm. Then, in early August, Blackbeard returned to sea.

On 11 August Governor Keith of Pennsylvania issued a warrant for the arrest of Teach, and it seems the pirate was accused of harassing local trading ships in Delaware Bay. Blackbeard mightn't have crossed the line into piracy yet, but intimidating traders to relinquish provisions was coming very close to it. He may well have attacked other ships – Captain Johnson suggests as much – but in late August he fell in with two French merchant ships, heading north from the Caribbean. He gave chase and captured them both. One vessel was fully laden, while the other was just carrying ballast. He moved the crew of the laden ship into her consort, and then let the second ship go. Blackbeard then sailed his prize to Ocracoke, where he spent most of September stripping her of her cargo and transferring it to a warehouse outside Bath Town rented to him for the purpose by Tobias Knight.

This was a risky venture, so he covered his tracks by claiming that he found the French ship abandoned on the high seas. According to Admiralty law this gave Teach salvage rights to the vessel. The trouble was, this fabrication needed to stand up in court. Fortunately Governor Eden either believed Teach, or turned a blind eye. As the Admiralty's representative in North Carolina he convened an Admiralty Court, and Teach was granted salvage rights.

It may have helped Teach's case that the local Admiralty representatives could claim a fifth of the cargo for themselves – a fee designed to offset administrative costs. Blackbeard duly delivered 80 barrels of sugar and cocoa to Eden and Knight. The rest of the cargo was sold in Bath Town, and the profits divided among Blackbeard's crew. Meanwhile the remaining French ship sailed into Philadelphia and reported what had happened. It was clear to everyone outside North Carolina that Teach was nothing more than an unreformed pirate. Something clearly had to be done.

**LATE JUNE
1718**

**Teach accepts
pardon from
Governor Eden**

**LATE AUGUST
1718**

**Teach captures two
French ships**

**EARLY NOVEMBER
1718**

**Governor
Spotswood plans
Blackbeard raid**

Governor Spotswood was incensed by the news, but what disturbed him even more was the report that Blackbeard had established a base on Ocracoke Island. This gave him a secure and remote base from which to operate, while still being close enough to Bath Town to sell his plunder to local merchants and unscrupulous local ship owners. Worse, there were reports that the diehard Captain Charles Vane had visited Ocracoke during his cruise off the Carolinas. Charles Vane's sloop *Ranger* – the one that had fired on Governor Rogers two months before – put in to Ocracoke, and the two pirate crews held a week-long party.

To Spotswood this made Blackbeard doubly dangerous. It raised the possibility that Ocracoke would become a bustling pirate haven, attracting the very pirates who had refused the pardon. The Outer Banks lay close to the Virginia Capes, and so pirates based there could lie off the Virginia coast, plundering at will. If threatened they could easily evade any larger pursuers in the shallow waters of Pamlico Sound. In Pennsylvania Governor Keith fitted out two sloops for anti-piracy patrol duties in Delaware Bay. Governor Johnson of South Carolina did the same. By October these sloops were at sea, but no pirates were encountered.

In Williamsburg, capital of the Virginia colony, Governor Spotswood had another solution. As early as July he had issued a proclamation requiring all former pirates – pardoned or not – to register with the colony's authorities. This was because Blackbeard's former crewmen – the men stranded at Topsail Inlet – were starting to drift into American ports, including Virginia ones. Laws were passed to prevent them from congregating, and one of them, William Howard, was arrested. He was Teach's former quartermaster from the *Queen Anne's Revenge*, and although he would eventually walk free, no doubt he also told the authorities as much as he could about the pirate captain who had stranded him and sailed off with the plunder.

Alexander Spotswood, a man of action – he was a former colonel in the British Army – had in 1710 become the Lieutenant Governor of Virginia, deputy to Governor Hamilton, Earl of Orkney. However, Hamilton was an absentee governor, and so Spotswood ruled the colony in his stead. His many duties included overseeing the Virginia militia, and under his tutelage they became an effective and well-disciplined force. Faced with Blackbeard, Governor Spotswood had bided his time, but in October he made his move. He decided to put the Virginia militiamen to good use.

What he planned was effectively an invasion. North Carolina wasn't a crown colony like Virginia, but it still proudly maintained its independence from its larger neighbours. A century and a half later, America was to tear itself apart over states' rights. In order to deal with Blackbeard, Spotswood had to send his militiamen over the border, and – as he put it – 'expurgate the nest of vipers'. This was all very well, but Blackbeard had a sloop, and could easily evade capture. That was why the attack had to be two-pronged – a march overland to capture the pirates in Bath Town, and a seaborne attack on Blackbeard's sloop off Ocracoke.

Fortunately for Spotswood, two British warships were lying at anchor in the James River, some 30 miles downstream from Williamsburg. On

Wednesday 13 November Captain Ellis Brand of the frigate HMS *Pearl* and Captain George Gordon of the smaller frigate HMS *Lyme* were summoned to Williamsburg by the governor, who met them in his partially completed palace. In theory neither captain was answerable to the colonial governor. They answered only to the Admiralty in London. Spotswood was answerable to the king through the Board of Trade. However, the frigates were there to protect the colony from attack by pirates, and both naval officers were willing to stretch their orders as far as they could, in order to deal with the threat posed by Blackbeard. With that problem sorted out, Spotswood and the two captains began planning the raid.

Despite the political furore it would cause, the planning of the land invasion was the easiest part. Captain Brand would lead a joint force of 100 Virginia militia and 100 armed sailors, and march them across country from the James River to Bath Town. When this force crossed the boundary

This chart of Pamlico Sound dating from the 1770s shows the intricate nature of this inland waterway, filled with sandbars and shoals. Bath Town is in the top left corner, Topsail Inlet is in the bottom left, and Ocracoke Island lies to the north of Ocracoke Inlet, which is clearly marked in the centre of the chart.

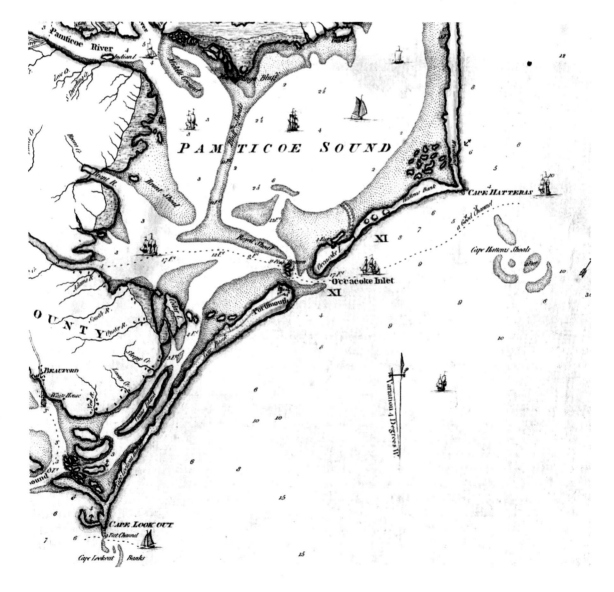

The small sloop shown here is similar in size to the *Ranger*. The *Jane* was slightly larger, and probably resembled the one in the background, lying over on her starboard side being careened. Both sloops were fast, manoeuvrable and shallow-draughted.

line between the two colonies Spotswood's authority would cease, and so Brand would have to deal with any diplomatic incidents that arose. He would also have to use his initiative when it came to rounding up the pirates in Bath Town, and confiscating any of their plunder.

Solid intelligence was hard to come by – Blackbeard and the bulk of his men could either be in Bath Town or off Ocracoke. However, it was thought most likely that they would be in the town. The expedition leaders had to be prepared for every eventuality. This was particularly true for the seaborne element, as it might be called upon to fight Blackbeard's sloop the *Adventure*, chase it if it tried to escape, or round up the pirates if they were camped on the island. Both naval officers knew that the waters inside the Outer Banks were far too shallow for their frigates. Therefore they suggested that Spotswood hire two civilian sloops, which they could then crew with their own men.

This was duly done, and the small vessels *Ranger* and *Jane* were sent out to the frigates' anchorage off Kecoughtan (now Hampton, Virginia). Lieutenant Robert Maynard, first lieutenant of the *Pearl*, was given command of the two craft, which were to be crewed by 32 men from the *Pearl*, who crewed the *Jane*, and 24 from the *Lyme*, who were sent into the *Ranger*. They were accompanied by one of the *Lyme*'s midshipmen, Mr Hyde, who would command the second sloop. Maynard himself took command of the slightly larger *Jane*. Finally, two local pilots were hired, one for each vessel, whose knowledge of the waters of Pamlico Sound would prove extremely useful. Counting Maynard himself, this meant the two sloops carried 60 men between them plus any civilian crew.

Maynard's orders were to navigate their way through Ocracoke Inlet and capture any pirates they could find on the island. He would then cross the 50 miles of Pamlico Sound and enter the Pamlico River. Once in place he would blockade the river, hopefully trapping Blackbeard's *Adventure* in Bath Creek. They would act as a floating reserve for Captain Brand's force, who would sweep in from the landward side. If everything went according to plan the pirates would be caught in a trap. Naturally they would fight, and Maynard had to be ready to thwart any attempt by the pirates to escape by sea. However, as nobody knew exactly where Blackbeard was, Maynard had to rely on his initiative, and stand ready to do battle with the pirates wherever they might be. When fighting a dangerous and wily man like Blackbeard, nothing could be taken for granted.

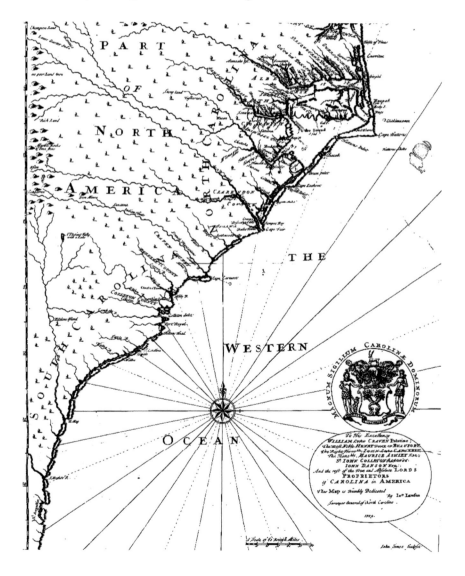

In this mid-18th-century chart of the Carolina coast the geographical layout of the Outer Banks is readily apparent – a winding barrier of islands lying between the Atlantic Ocean and the shallow inshore waters of Pamlico Sound. Ocracoke lies at the end of the dotted NNE projection of the compass rose.

THE RAID

Attacking the viper's nest

During the first days of November the men of the *Pearl* and the *Lyme* readied themselves for action. First there were the two sloops to prepare, and then the naval contingent of the invasion force. Boats must have been ferrying between the four vessels for most of that weekend, and the scene would have been one of bustle and disciplined activity. Captain Brand and his 100 armed sailors were given all the arms and provisions they needed, and meanwhile the two Virginia trading sloops, *Ranger* and *Jane*, which had come down from Jamestown on the James River had also brought the second half of Captain Brand's force – the 100 men of the Virginia militia. The old settlement of Jamestown served as the harbour for Williamsburg, as the colony's capital lay a few miles north of the James River. Williamsburg is where the militia were mustered and equipped.

Having been transported downriver the militia were landed at Portsmouth on the southern shore of the James River, while the senior officers went on board the *Pearl* to meet Captain Brand. Once the planned route of the march was mapped out the officers rejoined their men, while Brand and his naval contingent were ferried ashore to join them. Final preparations for the march would have been made there, and then with Brand in the lead, accompanied by local guides, the force would move off to the south-west, following the small dirt track that skirted the edge of the grimly named Dismal Swamp.

Back on board the *Lyme*, Lieutenant Maynard had finished the last entry in his journal before his two sloops set sail. It read:

> Mod[erate] gales & fair weather. This day I rec'd from Captain Gordon an order to command 60 men out of his Majesty's ships *Pearl* & *Lyme*, on board two small sloops, in order to destroy some pyrates, who resided in N. Carolina. This day weigh'd & sail'd hence with ye sloops under my command, having on board provisio of all species, with arms & ammunition suitable for ye occasion.

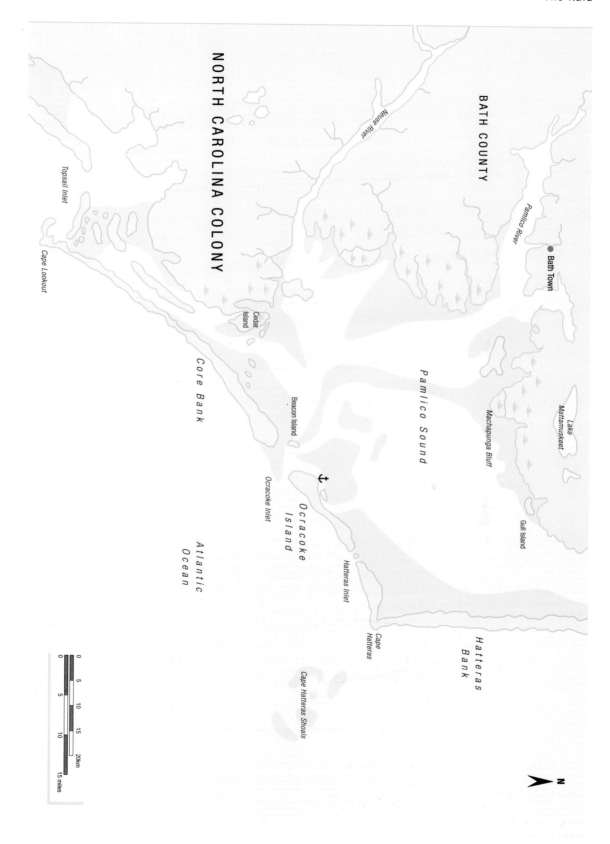

NORTH CAROLINA COLONY

BATH COUNTY

Neuse River

Pamlico River

● Bath Town

Lake
Mattamuskeet

Machapunga Bluff

Gull Island

Pamlico Sound

Topsail Inlet

Cape Lookout

Cedar
Island

Core Bank

Beacon Island

Ocracoke Inlet

Ocracoke
Island

Hatteras Inlet

Atlantic
Ocean

Cape
Hatteras

Hatteras
Bank

Cape Hatteras Shoals

N

0   5   10   15   20km
0   5   10   15 miles

This was an understatement. Although the sloops carried no cannon, the men were armed with a full arsenal of muskets, pistols, cutlasses, boarding pikes, boarding axes, daggers and *grenadoes* (grenades). As none of the men apart from the two officers wore any uniform they would have looked little different from the pirates they were being sent to attack.

What Maynard didn't record was that the original civilian crews of the two sloops remained on board them – or at least their masters did, and some of their crew. In 1721, when Captain Gordon of the *Lyme* recalled these preparations he noted that the two masters stayed aboard their vessels, and their crews made up 'a twelfth part of the whole number of men that went with them'. That meant that as well as his 56 seamen, two pilots and a midshipman, Maynard's force also included two civilian masters, and at least two other civilian seamen in each sloop. No doubt the vessels' owners wanted to make sure that their craft were returned intact.

As an added incentive, Governor Spotswood ensured that the Virginia legislature offered a bounty. Just before the sloops set sail Spotswood wrote to Captain Gordon, and laid out the terms of the arrangement. Sailors were perfectly used to receiving prize money when they captured an enemy ship in time of war, or in an anti-piracy action of this kind. The sailors would still receive a share of this reward if they captured Blackbeard's sloop, the *Adventure*, but now they would also get an added bonus based on the number of pirates they killed or captured.

The agreement read: 'For Edward Teach, commonly called Captain Teach or Blackbeard, one hundred pounds. For every other commander of a pyrate ship, sloop or vessel, forty pounds. For every Lieutenant, Master or Quartermaster, Boatswain or Carpenter twenty pounds. For every other inferior officer fifteen pounds, and for every private man taken on board such ship, sloop or vessel ten pounds.' This would have made the sailors even more eager for the fight that lay ahead of them.

Lieutenant Robert Maynard was an experienced naval officer, and as his small force got under way he must have contemplated what lay ahead. We don't know much about his early career, but he was born in Kent in 1683 or 1684, joined the Royal Navy as a teenager, and was serving as a midshipman when the War of the Spanish Succession broke out in 1701. He may well have been present at the capture of Gibraltar in 1704, and he certainly participated in the subsequent naval campaign fought out in the Mediterranean. He gained his commission as a lieutenant in Portsmouth on 14 January 1707, and two years later he appears in the naval records as the third lieutenant of the third-rate ship-of-the-line HMS *Bedford*, of 70 guns. At the time the *Bedford* formed part of the Channel Fleet, and in 1708 it saw action off Dunkirk before being despatched to the Mediterranean, where it joined the British fleet operating off the coast of Catalonia.

As naval careers go, Robert Maynard's progress up the promotion ladder was slow. This suggests he was an officer who lacked the patronage of a senior officer, or the family connections that could speed his advance through the service. His brother Thomas also joined the navy, and his progress was just as sluggish. However, by November 1718 the 35-year-old Robert Maynard was the first lieutenant of HMS *Pearl*, and therefore Captain Brand's second-in-command. He was seen as an extremely competent officer, and capable of commanding the frigate if his captain was absent from it. After his battle with Blackbeard Maynard's reputation was assured, and like his brother he ended his service career with the rank of captain, albeit as a master and commander – a captain who commanded a small warship, but who lacked full 'post captain' status.

In the evening watch (i.e. between 6pm and midnight) on Sunday 17 November the *Ranger* and the *Jane* parted company with the two frigates, and slipped out of the Kecoughtan anchorage. That first night they only travelled 20 nautical miles – a journey of less than three hours, given the fresh but weakening south-easterly winds reported in the *Pearl's* log book that evening. They dropped anchor in the lee of Cape Henry shortly before midnight, and spent the night riding at anchor in Lynnhaven Bay. They were at the mouth of Chesapeake Bay, and beyond the cape a mile to the west lay the rolling swell of the Atlantic.

When dawn broke the crews of the *Ranger* and the *Jane* ate breakfast, raised their anchors and headed out to sea, past the flat expanse of Cape Henry. The motion of the ships changed, as they were now heading at right angles to the swell, and virtually into the wind. This meant that progress would have been slow – the sloops were barely able to make five or six knots as they worked their way past what is now Virginia Beach. Maynard would also have ordered his two ships to separate. He didn't want the pirates to escape past him, and so he wanted his lookouts to be able to cover as large an area as they possibly could.

The standard procedure at this period was for a force of small ships to spread out, so that their lookouts could cover as wide an area of sea as possible. In ideal visibility a masthead lookout on a small sloop might be able to see an approaching ship from about 20 nautical miles away. However, the visibility that week wasn't particularly good – the logs of the ships in Kecoughtan reported rain showers. This meant that Maynard's men would have been lucky to see as far as 10 nautical miles. He would, therefore, have kept one sloop within 5 nautical miles of the coast, so they could spot any

Captain Johnson said of Teach that 'In time of action he wore a sling over his shoulders with three brace of pistols hanging in holsters, and stuck lighted matches under his hat, which, appearing on each side of his face, made him altogether such a figure that imagination cannot form any idea of a fury from hell to look more frightful'.

activity on the shore, and the other sloop would be stationed abreast of it, but further out to sea, just within visibility range. That meant that the two vessels could spot any ships approaching them within 20–25 nautical miles of the coast.

According to Maynard's report he managed to stop several coastal trading ships as he followed the coast as it fell away towards the south-south-east. From the master of one of these vessels, which had recently left Pamlico Sound, he learned that Blackbeard was no longer in Bath Town, but was on board the sloop *Adventure*, which was anchored in the lee of Ocracoke Island, on its western side. That meant that in a few days' time Maynard and his men faced the likelihood of a naval battle, fought out in the shallow waters and among the shifting sandbars found on that side of the island. While the pilots on both of his sloops knew the way through Ocracoke Inlet and the main channels of Pamlico Sound, Blackbeard and his men would have the advantage of local knowledge when it came to the waters off Ocracoke.

The voyage south took almost four days, with progress slowed by the fresh southerly wind and the rough, lumpy seas. Still, Maynard had taken these conditions into account when he made his plans, and so he arrived off Ocracoke Island when it was dark, a few hours after dusk fell on the evening of Thursday 21 November. There was an ebb tide, which meant that an attack that evening was all but impossible, as the two sloops would have to fight against the flood as they worked their way into Ocracoke Sound.

After consulting his pilot William Butler, Maynard decided to launch his attack shortly after dawn the following morning. No doubt he discussed the plan with Midshipman Hyde, and with his senior non-commissioned

The modern town of Ocracoke lies on the spur on the western or inner side of Ocracoke Island, in an area which, in 1718, was a mass of reed beds and marshy ground. In this view looking north, Teach's landing place lay on the far side of the tree-covered spur.

officers. Using a telescope Maynard could see the tips of the mast of what must be Blackbeard's sloop as it lay at anchor beyond the low-lying sand dunes that covered much of Ocracoke Island. He was unsure of it, but he suspected there might be another vessel anchored there too. This meant that the news passed on to him by the passing trading vessel's master was correct – Blackbeard and his sloop were at Ocracoke rather than at Bath Town. That in turn meant that the following morning Maynard and his men would be doing battle with the pirates.

The battle of Ocracoke Island

Ocracoke Island was shaped a bit like a human thigh bone – a femur. The island was about 15 miles long, with a rounded headland at each end, resembling the head and neck of the femur. This long thin island lay on a north-east to south-westerly axis, with its easterly side facing the Atlantic Ocean, and the western coast bordering the more sheltered waters of Pamlico Sound. In the femur there is a protuberance called the greater trochanter, which sticks out slightly from the rest of the bone. This resembles the small triangular part of the island that protrudes slightly into Pamlico Sound, on the western side of the island. This is the place where the town of Ocracoke stands today. In November 1718 there was nothing on the whole island except sand dunes, marram grass, scrub and low trees. Blackbeard's sloop was anchored close to this triangle of land, less than 2 nautical miles from the southern tip of the island.

Maynard heaved to a mile or two off this southern tip, close to the seaward approaches to Ocracoke Inlet, which formed the main shipping channel between the Atlantic and Pamlico Sound. He posted lookouts to watch for

The wind-ruffled waters of Pamlico Sound, viewed from the western shoreline of Ocracoke Island. In the distance the trees on the western spur of the island can be seen, hiding Ocracoke town, which lies beyond them. Thatch's Hole lies off to the left of this viewpoint.

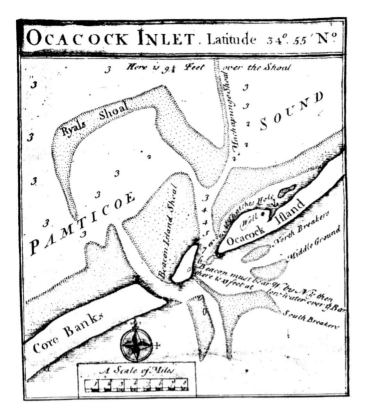

Ocracoke Inlet ran between Ocracoke Island to the north and Beacon Island to the south. The pirates' landing place on the island is marked here as Thatch's Hole. This chart also shows the dangerous sandbars that surrounded the narrow channel.

any sign of activity on the shore or on the pirate sloop. They would also have been told to keep an eye out to sea as well, as Maynard wanted to make sure that no ships would arrive unexpectedly during the night. These could easily rouse the pirates, or even warn them that the navy was about to attack them.

It was fortunate that Blackbeard hadn't posted any lookouts on the shore. If he had they would have surely spotted the two sloops, anchored in deep water a mile or so away to the south-east. The fact that the pirates were taken completely by surprise suggests that Blackbeard hadn't bothered to take this basic precaution. Just as importantly, he hadn't taken the equally important precautionary measures of keeping his sloop ready for action, with powder and shot placed close to her eight guns, and cutlasses, pistols, grenadoes and boarding axes close at hand, in case the pirates were taken unawares. Either Teach had become complacent after so many months of relative inactivity or else he was unable to convince his hard-drinking crew to take such duties seriously.

They were certainly drinking heavily that night. While Maynard's men were having a cold meal of beef and ship's biscuits washed down with spirit, beyond the far side of the island Blackbeard was entertaining a handful of guests. A small trading craft was anchored close to the *Adventure*, in the lee of Ocracoke Island, and at least two of her crew were on board the pirate sloop, drinking rum with Blackbeard and his crew. The same two unfortunate seamen were still on board the vessel when Maynard launched his attack the following morning. In his account of Edward Teach, Captain Johnson claims that Blackbeard entertained the sloop's master and three of her crew that evening. If this was true then by the end of the evening two of them were too drunk to make it back to their own ship.

During his time in these waters the *Adventure* and her crew had become a familiar sight to local coastal traders and fishermen, and this sort of fraternization was probably a regular occurrence. The small trading sloop had sailed from Bath Town that morning, and as well as her normal cargo – if she carried any – she bore a letter for Teach, written by Tobias Knight, Governor Eden's deputy. The next day the letter fell into the hands of Lieutenant Maynard, who in turn passed it on to his captain and then to Governor Spotswood. It is worth quoting this intriguing document in full:

My dear friend,

If this finds you yet in harbour I would have you make the best of your way up as soon as possible your affairs will let you. I have something more to say to you than at present I can write. The bearer will tell you the end our Indian warr, and Ganet can tell you in part what I have to say to you, so referr you in some measure to him.

I really think these three men are heartily sorry at their difference with you, and will be very willing to ask your pardon. I may advice, be ffreinds again, [as] its better than falling out among our selves.

I expect the Governor this night or tomorrow, who I believe would be likewise glad to see you before you goe – I have not the time to add save my healthy respects to you, and am your real friend and servant,

T. Knight

Clearly Tobias Knight had some important news to pass on to Blackbeard, but was unwilling to put it in a letter. It is entirely possible that Knight had received word that the governor of Virginia was planning to attack Bath Town, and consequently he sent a trusted advisor – Mr Ganet – to bring the pirate the news. The suggestion that he and Blackbeard had a falling out may indicate that Ganet was once a member of Blackbeard's crew, or that there had been some local disagreement, which Knight was eager to resolve. Tobias Knight's letter is deliberately ambiguous, but it certainly demonstrates that Knight and Teach were friends, and that Blackbeard was planning to leave the colony for a while – possibly on another pirate cruise.

In any case it seems unlikely that this letter of warning – if indeed it was one – included any indication that a naval force was on its way to attack the pirates. The sudden arrival of Maynard's sloops the following morning came as a complete surprise to Blackbeard and his men.

This armed sloop, anchored off Boston Light in 1729, is similar in size and appearance to Blackbeard's vessel *Adventure*. The only real difference was that in the *Adventure*, as in most pirate vessels, the quarterdeck would have been lowered, to provide a clear fighting area fore and aft.

THE BATTLE OF OCRACOKE

22 NOVEMBER 1718

This purely naval engagement was fought in the narrow navigable channel to the west of Ocracoke Island, a waterway bordered on the western side by a long line of sandbanks and shallows. Having arrived off the island the previous evening, Maynard was surprised to see Blackbeard's sloop the *Adventure* at anchor on the far side of the island. He decided to launch a dawn attack, hoping to catch the pirates by surprise. Lieutenant Maynard's two ships, the *Jane* and the *Ranger*, lacked any armament, and as Blackbeard's sloop *Adventure* was known to carry eight guns Maynard was also eager to close the range as quickly as possible.

As dawn broke (5.30am) *Jane* and *Ranger* were riding at anchor, approximately 1 nautical mile to seaward of the southern tip of Ocracoke Island, near the entrance to Ocracoke Inlet. After a cold breakfast the two crews recovered their anchors and prepared for battle. At approximately 6.30am they got under way, proceeding towards the inlet in line astern, with the *Jane* in the lead. The wind was light, from the south-west, and the sea was calm.

This reconstruction of the engagement is based upon an appraisal of all available sources. Where these are unclear or contradictory, the sailing performance of the vessels and local conditions have been used to determine the most likely course of action by the various participants. The vessels have been illustrated at a much bigger size than the scale would suggest, in order to make the distinction between the ships clearer, and their alignments more evident.

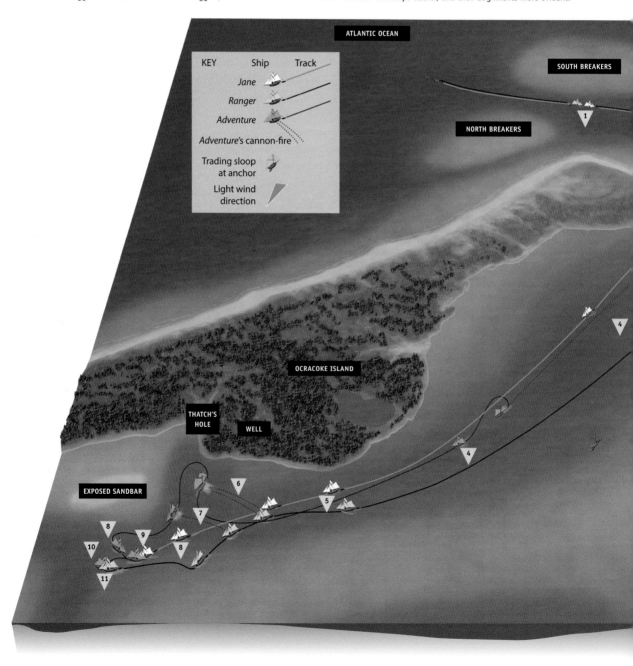

▼ EVENTS

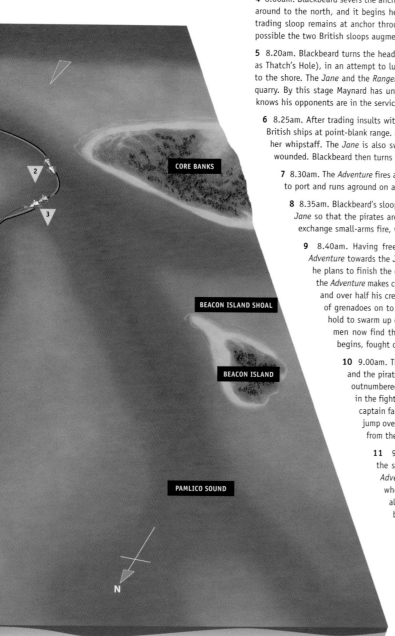

1 7.00am. The *Jane* crews her small longboat, which rows ahead of the two sloops; the longboat's crew take depth soundings using a sounding lead. The *Ranger* tows her own longboat astern of her. In this fashion Maynard's force slowly enters Ocracoke Inlet.

2 7.30am. The *Jane*'s longboat rounds the southern tip of Ocracoke Island, and minutes later she is spotted by a pirate lookout on board the *Adventure*. Minutes later the two British sloops also round the point. Maynard also sights the *Adventure* lying at anchor in front of the western spur of Ocracoke Island; another civilian sloop is seen at anchor to the west of her.

3 7.35am. The longboat is fired upon by the *Adventure*. At this point Maynard recovers the *Jane*'s boat crew, and tows the longboat astern of his vessel. This done, the sloops continue up the narrow channel leading towards Teach's anchorage, with the *Ranger* forming up on the port beam of the *Jane*.

4 8.00am. Blackbeard severs the anchor cable of the *Adventure* and raises sail. His sloop swings around to the north, and it begins heading directly away from her unidentified pursuers. The trading sloop remains at anchor throughout the ensuing battle. To close the range as fast as possible the two British sloops augment their sails with sweeps (oars).

5 8.20am. Blackbeard turns the head of the *Adventure* towards the landing place (now known as Thatch's Hole), in an attempt to lure the British sloops on to a sandbar which runs parallel to the shore. The *Jane* and the *Ranger* continue to close the distance between them and their quarry. By this stage Maynard has unfurled the Union flag from his masthead, so Blackbeard knows his opponents are in the service of the British Crown.

6 8.25am. After trading insults with Maynard, Blackbeard fires a starboard broadside at the British ships at point-blank range. Midshipman Hyde of the *Ranger* is killed, as is the man at her whipstaff. The *Jane* is also swept by grapeshot, and several of her crew are killed or wounded. Blackbeard then turns the *Adventure* away from the beach.

7 8.30am. The *Adventure* fires a port broadside at the *Ranger*; badly hit, the *Ranger* veers to port and runs aground on a shoal.

8 8.35am. Blackbeard's sloop temporarily runs aground, and Maynard manoeuvres the *Jane* so that the pirates are unable to fire another broadside at her. The two crews exchange small-arms fire, while Maynard waits for the *Ranger* to rejoin the fight.

9 8.40am. Having freed his sloop from the sandbar, Blackbeard steers the *Adventure* towards the *Jane*. He can only see a handful of men on her deck, and he plans to finish the enemy off by boarding Maynard's vessel. The port bow of the *Adventure* makes contact with the starboard bow of the *Jane*, and Blackbeard and over half his crew jump aboard the British sloop, after launching a salvo of grenadoes on to her deck. Maynard orders the men he has hidden in the hold to swarm up out of the hold and join in the fight. Blackbeard and his men now find themselves outnumbered, as a brutal hand-to-hand fight begins, fought out on the forward deck of the *Jane*.

10 9.00am. The lines securing the *Adventure* to the *Jane* are severed, and the pirate sloop drifts away from the smaller vessel. Blackbeard's outnumbered crew are forced back towards the bow of the *Jane*, and in the fighting Blackbeard is wounded, and then killed. Seeing their captain fall, the remainder of his boarding party either surrender or jump overboard, where after begging for quarter they are recovered from the water and taken prisoner.

11 9.05am. The *Ranger*, having now freed herself from the sandbar, manoeuvres alongside the starboard side of the *Adventure*. Her crew quickly overpower the ten pirates who have remained on board. As the *Jane* manoeuvres alongside the *Adventure*'s port side a pirate attempting to blow up the *Adventure* is overpowered, and the battle comes to an end.

Although this naval gun depicted in John Sellar's *The Sea Gunner* (1691) is a 12-pounder, and therefore a much larger weapon than the guns mounted on Blackbeard's sloop *Adventure*, the proportions and appearance of the gun and the carriage would have been similar.

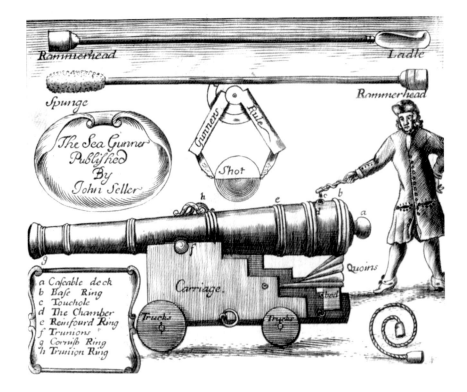

That night the *Adventure* only had a skeleton crew aboard. Blackbeard's first mate Israel Hands was in Bath Town, with 24 of the pirate crew. That left just Blackbeard and 25 men aboard the sloop. That, though, was more than the number he brought with him from Topsail Inlet, which suggests that he had been recruiting since he arrived in Bath Town, or possibly that a number of Blackbeard's former shipmates had arrived in the area, had forgiven Teach for abandoning them, and had rejoined his crew. This may well account for the bad feeling between Blackbeard and Ganet mentioned in Knight's letter, and why the traders were so willing to consort with the pirates that evening. Others of his original crew might also have drifted away after Blackbeard accepted the pardon, as they felt the life of a law-abiding seaman held little appeal for them. In any case, when dawn broke the pirates would find themselves outnumbered by more than two to one.

The log books of the *Pearl* and the *Lyme* reveal that in the mouth of the James River dawn on Friday 22 November ushered in a grey overcast day, with almost no wind, and the lumpy seas of the past few days had given way to calm ones. We can assume that 120 nautical miles to the south the morning was a similar one, as Lieutenant Maynard claims as much in his report. Dawn came at around 6.30am that morning. The British sailors had been roused an hour before, and had eaten a cold but hearty breakfast. Just like the evening before, no cooking fires were lit for fear the smoke might be seen by the pirates. Maynard would then have passed the order to his men to prepare for battle. Almost certainly there was nothing much to do – there were no guns to run out, and the crews of the two sloops had effectively been ready for action since the previous evening. Similarly, however hard they might have tried, many of Maynard's 60 crewmen would have had trouble sleeping during the night, as they knew that in the morning they could well be fighting for their very lives.

Both of the two British sloops were towing a small ship's boat behind them, probably 18ft four-oared longboats. Maynard ordered one of these to be crewed, and for it to take station ahead of the two sloops. His intention was to creep into Ocracoke Inlet, with the longboat leading the way. Its five-man crew were equipped with a sounding line, and they would take soundings as the procession of ships entered the narrow twisting channel. It was now 7.00am, and for the next half an hour the force moved quietly onward. The water in the main channel was approximately 6 fathoms (36ft) deep at low water, and the sloops drew less than 8ft. However, on either side of the channel were sandbars and shoals, whose position shifted with every

In this dramatic depiction by Howard Pyle of Blackbeard's last fight, the pirate can be seen locked in his duel with Lieutenant Maynard. Although it is historically inaccurate – for instance, pirates never wore headscarves – it vividly captures the brutal nature of the fighting.

storm. Maynard was right to be cautious – to have one of his sloops run aground at this stage would have spelt disaster.

The *Adventure* lay at anchor off the southern edge of the flat triangular spur on the island where the little town and harbour of Ocracoke stands today. On the far side of the spur lay the landing place the pirates used when they wanted to go ashore, or to refill their water casks from the island's spring. The southern tip of the island was 2 miles away, at the end of a relatively deep channel, which ran between the island on one side and a long sandbank on the other. It must have been about 7.30am when the small longboat first rounded the headland, and was spotted by the pirates. They would also have seen the two masts of Maynard's ships, rising from beyond the low-lying headland, and moving slowly forwards into the entrance to the channel.

As there was an incoming tide the bows of the *Adventure* were pointing south, directly towards the approaching enemy. It was claimed that Blackbeard fired off one of his guns as a warning shot, but given the direction his sloop was facing that would have been difficult. The pirate

In the early 18th century Ocracoke Island was typical of the barrier islands of the Outer Banks – long, thin and devoid of habitation. It was covered in sand dunes, marram grass and scrub, with some reed beds on its inner side, facing Pamlico Sound.

sloop carried eight main guns, with four guns to each broadside. These would have been facing the wrong way when the longboat came in sight, so a shot from them wouldn't have scared anybody. However, while Maynard's report lists eight guns on board, a copy of it published in the *British Gazette* listed nine guns. While one of these could have been a small swivel gun, if the ninth gun existed it would have been carried as a bow chaser, mounted in the forecastle of the pirate sloop. In any event it was probably the pirate master gunner, Philip Morton, who fired this first shot, at about 7.35am.

If this warning shot was fired by a 4-pounder gun, then it barely had the range to reach the longboat. If a larger 6-pounder was used then the shot could easily have whistled over the heads of the longboat crew. Whatever the size of shot the pirates used, an impressive waterspout would have been created, and the boat's crew would certainly have got the message. If they came closer the next shot would be both in range and on target. It was just as likely, though, that Morton fired a swivel gun. The longboat crew would have heard the shot, and realized the pirates had spotted them. A swivel gun was a light anti-personnel weapon, about the same size as a modern machine gun. It was quick to load and easy to aim and fire – you simply pointed the gun at the enemy using an iron 'tiller' or handle, and clapped a piece of burning slow-match into the touch-hole of the powder chamber.

These swivel guns were mounted on the ship's rail – in this case probably on the forecastle or quarterdeck – and they were loaded with either scrap metal or musket balls. They had a range of about 60 yards, and if fired in the last

moments before a boarding action could be very deadly. At this range though, they were merely a noisy way of warning the boat crew off.

At this time the pirates had no idea who these newcomers were. Morton had fired the traditional shot across the bows, and now Blackbeard and his crew watched and waited, to see what would happen next. The two sloops then emerged from behind the headland, and lingered there for a few moments as Maynard took the boat crew back on board, then towed the small craft astern of

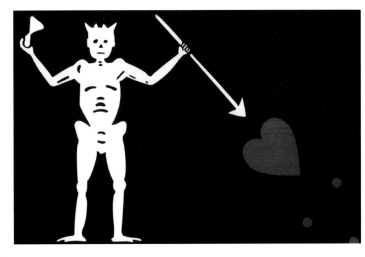

him. At this point the *Jane* was ahead of the *Ranger*, and for a professional naval crew the whole process of recovering the crew would have taken no more than a couple of minutes. It was therefore about 7.40am.

Blackbeard and his men would have peered in vain for any flag. In the age of fighting sail it was normal for warships to unfurl their colours before they opened fire, but it was perfectly acceptable to hide your identity until the last moment. In many cases captains flew false colours, to keep their enemy guessing. Any trick that helped to delay the enemy opening fire was considered fair game. In this battle, neither Maynard nor Hyde raised their Union flags to the masthead until they were in musket range – within 150 yards of the pirates.

When the two sloops continued to close the distance Blackbeard was forced to take action. Given the wind and tidal conditions that morning it would take Maynard around 20 minutes to reach the *Adventure*. This didn't give the pirates enough time to recover their anchor, even though the sloop lay in just 36ft of water. The anchor was firmly embedded in the sand-covered bottom, with around 70ft of cable laid out. To man the capstan and winch in the thick rope anchor cable would simply have taken too long – the pirates would still be manning the capstan when the sloop reached them.

Blackbeard adopted a much simpler solution – he cut the cable. This sounds drastic, but as an experienced seamen Teach was probably ready for this sort of eventuality. He would have had a marker buoy ready, which he would have secured to the remains of the anchor cable. Once the oncoming sloops had been dealt with he would then be able to come back and recover the anchor. When the cable was cut the *Adventure* would have swung round into the wind until she was facing the island. She would also have drifted slightly to port, away from the approaching sloops. Then, a minute or two later the pirates would have raised their two sails, and the head of the *Adventure* would have turned to port, spinning past the spur of the island until it was facing towards the sandbanks of Pamlico Sound. Somewhere close by was the trading sloop, which remained resolutely at anchor as the pirates slipped past them.

This is a reconstruction of Blackbeard's personal version of the pirate 'Jolly Roger', which he flew when he chased a potential prize. It served as a warning of the dangers of resisting his attack. Pirates frequently made use of skeletons as well as skulls and crossed bones.

At this point Blackbeard had a decision to make. He could have taken advantage of both his shallow draught and local knowledge, and threaded his way through the sandbar into Pamlico Sound. There were other small channels through the barrier islands, and the *Adventure* could well have slipped through one of them to reach the safety of the Atlantic. Once there he would probably have been able to evade his pursuers and escape. Blackbeard might have considered this option, but it wasn't in his nature to run from a fight. He therefore decided to fight the attackers, regardless of the odds or who they might be. This, he would have realized, would be a fight to the death, with no quarter asked for or given. From what we know of Teach he would have relished the prospect.

Blackbeard had one big advantage over his two opponents. Not only was the *Adventure* larger than the *Jane* and the *Ranger*, she was also armed with guns. Given the width of the channel, Maynard's two sloops had little option but to sail straight towards the pirate vessel. Blackbeard planned to let rip with a full broadside at close range, and then keep pounding away with his guns. Once he had weakened both of the attacking sloops he could then come alongside them one at a time, and board them at cutlass-point. Edward Teach, the most notorious pirate in the Americas, would emerge victorious or die in the attempt.

Philip Morton would have made sure that the pirate sloop's battery of main guns were primed and loaded. In some cases this could have been done a few days before, and the guns could be double-shotted or even triple-shotted, for maximum effect. The gunner would have left them this way as a precaution, with covers over the gun muzzles and lead patches over the touch-holes to keep the powder dry. Even then, the guns would still have to be wormed out once a week, and the powder replaced, just to make sure. This was a standard precaution in merchant ships when sailing through dangerous waters, or in a warship expecting imminent action. One of the guns recovered from the wreck of *Queen Anne's Revenge* was loaded in this fashion, so the pirates certainly used their guns this way when they wanted to.

This though, required a level of discipline and commitment that probably didn't exist on board the smaller pirate vessel. If that was the case Morton would have spent the next 15 minutes or so frantically supervising the loading of his guns, and generally preparing them for the battle ahead. Unfortunately we don't even know exactly how big these guns were. A naval sloop of the period – the Royal Navy called them 'cutters' – would have typically carried eight 3-pounders. Each barrel would have been produced from cast iron, and would have been 5ft 6in long, mounted on a small four-wheeled carriage with solid wooden trucks or wheels. Each barrel would have weighed 7 cwt (784lb), which if well mounted would have been light enough to be crewed by four men.

However, Blackbeard's old flagship *Queen Anne's Revenge* carried a range of guns, including 4-pounders and 6-pounders, the latter having 8ft-long barrels and weighing 22 cwt (2,464lb) apiece. Normally guns of this size weren't carried in sloops, as the guns would have been so heavy they would have impaired the sailing qualities of the ship, and the recoil would place too great a strain on the ship's timbers when they were fired. Like most pirates Teach probably didn't care too much about the strain on his vessel's hull. After all, he could easily capture another ship. However, he did consider speed to be important, and while he might conceivably have included one or two 6-pounders in his main battery, the chances were the sloop was armed with smaller 3- or 4-pounder weapons.

Both Teach and Morton knew that the effective range of a 4-pounder was about 1,000 yards, or half a nautical mile. Maximum range would have been double that – the official maximum range at 10 degrees of elevation was given as 1,920 yards. This, though, was all theoretical. What the pirates wanted was to wait until the range was so close they couldn't miss. That meant holding fire until the enemy got within half of the effective range – less than 500 yards. At that range the pirates' guns – let's assume they were 4-pounders – would have been highly effective. They would have been especially so as the two naval ships were approaching the *Adventure* at right angles, so the pirate shot would have been passing down the length of the naval vessel. This – a 'raking shot' – would have been devastating, as the 3in-diameter iron ball would have smashed into the bow of one of the vessels, and then passed down its entire length, mangling anything that lay in its path – masts, superstructure or sailors.

Strangely, Blackbeard didn't fire at this range, but waited until the sloops came much closer. The gunnery tables of the period list the 'point blank' range of the 4-pounder as 120 yards. It seems as if Morton had loaded at least some of his guns with grapeshot rather than solid round shot. Grapeshot consisted of musket balls and scrap metal put into cloth bags that disintegrated when fired, scattering their contents, a bit like a larger version of the charge loaded into swivel guns. The effective range of grapeshot fired from a 4-pounder was under 250 yards, as these were anti-personnel charges. The devastation caused when the *Adventure* finally unleashed her broadside suggests that Morton had chosen to use grape. At point-blank range these musket balls and scraps of metal would scythe through the men lining the bulwarks of the enemy ship, cutting them down as if they'd been fired at by a company of musket-armed soldiers. It was the perfect tool for this kind of grisly work.

While the pirates were preparing their guns and getting their sloop under way, Maynard's two craft were closing the range as quickly as they could. After all, they were sailing directly into the guns of the pirate ship, and a raking shot at this stage could have ended the battle before it began. It would have taken them 15 minutes to get within 500 yards of the *Adventure*, and by this time the pirates were on the move, slipping around the spur of Ocracoke Island towards the landing place beyond it.

While many of the accounts claim that Maynard sent part of his crew below decks during the battle, it makes much more sense if this happened before they closed with the pirates. That way the men would have been hidden from sight, and would enjoy some protection from incoming shot. Maynard reported that the hatch covers were removed and extra ladders were fitted, which suggests this was a ploy he had planned carefully, rather

In this detail from the popular painting by J. L. G. Ferris entitled 'The Capture of the Pirate Blackbeard, 1718', the two rival captains are shown locked in their own private duel, while a British seaman – presumably Abraham Demelt – is shown with his cutlass poised, ready to slash Blackbeard across the face and neck.

than a spur of the moment idea. Once he came alongside the *Adventure* these hidden men could race up the ladders and take the pirates by surprise. If it was all part of Maynard's plan he would have hidden all but a dozen of the men before they came close enough for individuals to be seen.

Maynard remained on deck, as did the pilot and the helmsman, who stood beside the whipstaff – the steering tiller that operated the *Jane*'s rudder. Maynard would have stood next to him, to whisper orders during the approach. Midshipman Hyde would have taken up the same position aboard the *Ranger*. Captain Johnson also claims that Maynard's men used their oars or sweeps to speed their progress in these light airs. This made perfect sense, as the aim was to close the deadly gap in front of the *Adventure*'s guns in as short a time as possible. Sweeps would have been rigged, and at least eight of the crew would have been on hand to operate them on each vessel, to augment the power of the sails.

Soon the distance between the two sides had closed to within 150 yards. This was when Maynard gave the order to unfurl the Union flags carried at the masthead of both craft. By showing his colours he was making sure that the pirates knew exactly who he was. The newspapers reported that Blackbeard responded by unfurling his own pirate flag, but in all probability he didn't bother. His own version of the 'Jolly Roger' was a skeleton holding a spear, having just pierced a red heart. This was a flag designed to intimidate a merchant captain, not to fly in battle. While it might have been romantic to assume this flag was flown during Blackbeard's last fight, nobody who was there at the time ever mentioned it. Besides, Maynard's men weren't likely to be intimidated, and knew perfectly well who was in the sloop that lay ahead of them.

The *Adventure* had turned away from her pursuers, and was now heading back towards the shore of the island, with Blackbeard himself steering. His quartermaster, Thomas Miller, noticed that they were fast approaching the landing place – the small inlet now known as Teach's Hole where the pirates landed to refill their water barrels from a nearby spring. He tried to warn Blackbeard that the water was shoaling fast, and if he held his course they would run aground. Blackbeard merely pushed him roughly aside and sent him sprawling across the deck. He was entering these shallow waters deliberately, as he knew that a sandbar lay parallel to the beach, and he planned to lure his pursuers on to it, turning away into deeper water at the last minute. Then he could stand off from them and fire his guns into the stationary hulls. The range continued to close, but Blackbeard kept his nerve, and held his course.

By now the *Adventure* and the *Jane* were well within 100 yards of each other. The exchange that followed was quoted by Maynard in his report: 'At our first salutation he [Blackbeard] drank damnation to me and my men, whom he sti'led cowardly puppies, saying he would neither give nor take quarter'. This bears a ring of truth to it – the gap between the vessels was closing fast, Blackbeard had one eye on the approaching sandbar, and neither he nor Maynard seemed the type to have engaged in excessive talking. This didn't stop the brief exchange being augmented by the newspapers, and by Captain Johnson in his bestselling book. According to him, the exchange went like this:

> Blackbeard hailed him in his rude manner: 'Damn you for villains, who are you, and whence do you come?' The Lieutenant make him answer; 'You may see from our colours we are no pyrates.' Blackbeard bid him send his boat on board, that he may see who he was, but Mr. Maynard reply'd thus: 'I cannot spare my boat, but I will come aboard you as soon as I can with my sloop.' Upon this Blackbeard took a glass of liquor & drank him with these words; 'Damnation seize my soul if I give you quarter, or take any from you.' In answer to which, Mr. Maynard told him that he expected no quarter from him, nor should he give him any.

This was a colourful fabrication, but even the exchange recounted by Maynard was dramatic enough, given the circumstances. The exchange was probably even briefer than it might otherwise have been, as seconds later Blackbeard opened fire.

22 NOVEMBER 1718

**8.25am
Teach fires
broadside at *Jane*
and *Ranger***

In this depiction of Blackbeard used to illustrate the third edition of Captain Johnson's *General History of Pyrates*, Teach is shown sporting a fur cap – a common form of headgear worn by mariners of this period in inclement weather.

After the verbal exchange, Blackbeard pushed the whipstaff over and the *Adventure* heeled round, away from the fast-approaching sandbar. As the pirate sloop spun round her starboard battery of guns could finally bear on the British sloops, which by this stage were probably less than 100 yards away. The four little guns poured their broadside into the enemy, their weight of fire no doubt augmented by at least a couple of swivel guns, and probably musket fire for good measure. The pirates seem to have split their fire, as both of the naval sloops were hit by a blast of grapeshot. At that range it was almost impossible to miss.

In his after-action report, Maynard wrote: 'Immediately we engaged, and Mr. Hyde was unfortunately kill'd, and five of his men wounded in the little sloop, which, having nobody to command her, fell astern, and did not come up to assist me until the action was almost over'. He was understating the case. Here is how the *Boston News Letter* described the broadside:

> Then Lieutenant Maynard told his men that they knew what they had to do, and could not escape the pirates' hands if they had a mind, but must either fight or be killed. At that point Blackbeard opened fire. Teach begun and fired some small guns loaded with swan shot [grapeshot], spick nails, and pieces of old iron, in upon Maynard, which killed six of his men and wounded ten.

In his account Captain Johnson claimed that on board the *Jane* 20 of her crew were killed or wounded by the discharge, plus a further nine on the *Ranger*, including Mr Hyde, who was killed instantly. As Maynard only had 32 men on board the *Jane*, not counting the civilians, this accounted for almost half of his total force. The newspaper account seems more accurate, but still, if Maynard hid men below decks, then the claim is that this blast would have killed or incapacitated almost everyone who remained on deck. Maynard himself was lucky to have avoided being hit.

This, though, was probably an exaggeration. In his version of his subordinate's action, Captain Gordon reported to the Admiralty that during the battle 'the *Pearl* sloop [*Jane*] had killed and died of their wounds nine, my sloop [*Ranger*] had two killed, in both sloops there were upwards of twenty wounded'. Although he seems to have mixed up the two vessels, this official death toll was much lower than the one claimed in the press and by Johnson. If we accept that the nine casualties were inflicted on the *Ranger* rather than the *Jane*, then this ties in with the other accounts, particularly Maynard's own report. The lower casualty rate on the *Jane* also accords with Maynard's version, and with the way events unfolded over the next few minutes. We can therefore assume that while the *Ranger* was hit badly, the *Jane* escaped with relatively few casualties, largely as many of her crew were hiding below decks.

On the *Ranger* Maynard said that Midshipman Hyde was killed by the pirate broadside, and Johnson claims another eight crewmen fell with him – a tally borne out (with the proviso that he confused the two sloops) by Captain Brand. As the *Ranger* was crewed by 24 sailors from HMS *Lyme*, plus the midshipman and about four civilians, this was a very telling hit. In an instant, Maynard had lost anything between a third and a half of his entire force. Another similar broadside would be crippling, and would probably leave him with too few men to continue the fight. What is particularly impressive is the way the captain and crew of the *Jane* shrugged off their casualties, and continued to close with the enemy.

While the *Jane* was still giving chase, the pirate broadside effectively put the *Ranger* out of action. Not only was Midshipman Hyde killed, but it seems his senior ratings or petty officers fell as well, as Maynard described the smaller craft as having 'no-body to command her'. The helmsman was also cut down, and as a result the *Ranger* veered off course, and promptly ran aground on a sandbar. She would remain there for several crucial minutes, before the remainder of her crew could rally themselves, and work their ship back into the channel.

This is where the various accounts begin to differ. Captain Johnson claimed that Blackbeard's sloop also ran aground, and that Maynard then anchored within 'half a gunshot' of the pirates. Meanwhile his crew began lightening the vessel – throwing overboard anything they could to reduce the draught of their ship, so it could cross the shallows to reach the *Adventure*, which was now either aground on, or on the far side of, a sandbar. This makes little sense. It is highly unlikely that Maynard would have anchored within 50 yards of an enemy ship armed with guns, when his own vessel lacked any ordnance whatsoever. That would merely invite another crippling broadside fired at point-blank range. Also, Maynard made no mention of dropping anchor in his own report. While the *Ranger* and possibly also the *Jane* and the *Adventure* might have temporarily run aground, there is no hard evidence that Maynard did anything other than try to close with the enemy.

Another mystery surrounds the timing of Maynard's decision to hide a portion of his crew in the hold. The *Boston News Letter* claims that after the broadside, 'Lieutenant Maynard ordered all the rest of his men to go down in the hold. Himself, Abraham Demelt of New York and a third at the helm stayed above deck.' Captain Johnson – contradicting his own claim about coming to anchor – wrote that 'The lieutenant, finding his own ship had way, and would soon be on board of Teach, he ordered all his men down, for fear of another broadside'. None of this makes much sense. The whole point of hiding a portion of his crew was to surprise the pirates when the two ships came alongside each other. At this range any men on deck would have been clearly visible. Also, if we accept the relatively low casualty rate on board the *Jane*, then this also suggests that Maynard hid his men long before Blackbeard and his crew could see what was happening on the decks of the British sloop.

The claim that the *Adventure* ran aground is also open to doubt. The *British Gazetteer* quoted Maynard as saying that 'Continuing the fight, it being perfect calm, I shot away Teach's jib, and his fore halliards, forcing him ashoar'. This was nigh on impossible, as the *Jane* didn't carry any ordnance. While he might have cut the *Adventure*'s jib-sheet halliards with small-arms fire, or even a light swivel gun, this is unlikely. Besides, Maynard makes no mention of this in his report. The assumption is therefore that this was merely a quote added to spice up the newspaper's story. Several accounts suggest that the *Adventure* temporarily ran aground, but the reason for this is unclear. It might have been because her rigging was severed, because Blackbeard steered the wrong course, or possibly the recoil nudged her ashore as a result of firing a full broadside. Whatever the reason it seems that Blackbeard's sloop, the small *Ranger* and possibly also the *Jane* were stuck in the shallows.

It was now a race to see which of these three would free themselves first. The tide was still coming in, and so with each passing minute the water level was rising. This may have been why Maynard was said to have lightened his ship. However, to do so he would probably have had to call his men up from the hold, and therefore lose the element of surprise. It seems he didn't do this. This meant that either the *Jane* was still under way, or else if she did stick on the sandbar, Maynard was confident that the incoming tide would set his vessel free. It makes more sense that the panic to lighten ship would have taken place on the *Adventure* rather than the *Jane*.

This too fits in with the story about anchoring. Rather than dropping anchor, if the *Jane* was the only sloop capable of moving, then Maynard would have heaved to somewhere out of reach of the stranded *Adventure*'s guns, and the men left on deck would have opened fire with muskets and pistols. It was the cautious thing to do – an approach that must have appealed to Maynard. He could try to whittle down the number of men on Blackbeard's sloop, while keeping his own men under cover. The pirates would have been even more exposed if the *Adventure* was leaning over facing the British sloop, as the angle of her decks would have meant the bulwarks provided less cover than usual. This approach also bought a little more time for Maynard, who needed the support of the battered *Ranger* before he could risk boarding the pirate vessel.

Unfortunately for Maynard the *Adventure* was the first of the ships to free herself. To Blackbeard the *Jane* must have looked like an easy target. Very few men could be seen on her decks, and at least two of these were wounded. He still had the best part of 25 men at his disposal, and it looked as though they wouldn't have any problem overwhelming the *Jane*'s crew. Blackbeard could then turn his attention to the stricken *Ranger*. So far the battle had been going extremely well for the pirate captain. This, though, was the moment when he made his fatal mistake. Once the *Adventure* freed herself from the sandbar he could have manoeuvred the sloop round so that her guns could bear on the *Jane*. Then, after firing another broadside or two he could move alongside her, throw grenadoes on to her decks and then board her through the smoke. Teach must have been supremely over-confident, as instead of firing on his opponent he threw caution to the wind and set a course directly towards her.

The battle now entered its final phase. While up to now things had been going Teach's way, Maynard's plan was working. Blackbeard's sloop was approaching, and he still held his trump card – the body of well-armed sailors hiding in the hold of his small ship. He probably hoped he could surprise the initial wave of pirates, and then sever the boarding lines keeping the two vessels together. This would allow him to finish off Blackbeard and his boarders before turning his attention to the rest of the pirate crew. It was an excellent plan, but with the *Ranger* out of the fight Maynard needed to make the most of this surprise counter-attack.

As the *Adventure* came alongside the *Jane* Blackbeard ordered his men to throw a volley of grenadoes on to the enemy decks. A grenadoe was the forerunner of a modern grenade. It consisted of an empty cast-iron sphere the size of a round shot, filled with gunpowder. A rudimentary fuse was used to ignite the charge, and at the right moment these weapons could be thrown on to the decks of an enemy ship, where they would explode,

22 NOVEMBER 1718

8.40am
Teach boards the *Jane*

scattering pieces of the iron casing in all directions. Archaeological evidence has shown that similar projectiles could be made using empty glass or stoneware bottles, and these more rudimentary projectiles would be just as deadly as their purpose-built counterparts. Fortunately for Maynard none of the grenadoes were lobbed into the open hatch of the hold where most of his men were hidden.

Grappling hooks locked the two sloops together, making sure this would be a fight to the finish. It seems the bows of the ships were touching, and this was where the pirates were standing, ready to spring into action. As the smoke from the grenadoes still swirled over the *Jane*'s open deck, Blackbeard was heard to call out to his men that the enemy were 'all knocked on the head, except three or four ... let's jump on board and cut them to pieces'. With this Blackbeard and ten of his men jumped on to the *Jane*'s bulwarks, and then on to her forecastle.

The handful of defenders he saw – Robert Maynard, Abraham Demelt, the pilot William Butler and possibly one or two other British seamen – must have looked an insignificant group clustered on the deck of the *Jane*. Other wounded seamen – at least two, and possibly more – lay on the deck in front of them, amid the detritus of the grenado attack. Smoke would also have been swirling over the decks, from the grenadoes and from musket and pistol fire as the pirates who remained on the *Adventure* took aim at the small knot of British sailors. To Blackbeard, victory must have looked a certainty. Then, Maynard gave the signal for his men to race up the ladders from the hold.

In an instant the odds had changed. The sailors would have been yelling and shouting, and firing pistols at the pirates as they emerged from hiding. Here the accounts get confused again. Maynard, quoted in the *British Gazette*, said that Captain Teach attacked him with ten men, 'but [the] twelve men I left there fought like heroes, sword in hand'. In his version Captain Johnson claims Maynard commanded 12 men, and Blackbeard had 14. This all hinges on the number of casualties inflicted by Blackbeard's broadside. If Maynard lost ten men, then he would still be left with 25 crewmen, including the pilot and two or three Virginia traders.

This probably meant that the dozen men he mentioned were the number on deck at the time the pirates launched their attack. That left a similar number to race up from the hold. All the accounts agree that Blackbeard attacked with 10–14 men, leaving the rest on board the *Adventure* to protect the sloop, and to pour small-arms fire into the knot of defenders on the *Jane*. That means this battle – essentially the most important anti-piracy action of the period – was fought by just two dozen men per side. Both captains had already yelled out that they planned to offer no quarter – no chance for the enemy to surrender. All of these men – pirates, British seamen or Virginians – knew that they had to win or die.

Edward Teach typically armed himself with several pairs of pistols and a cutlass. Others were armed with whatever they were issued with or had within reach – pistols, cutlasses, boarding axes and half-pikes. Everyone had at least one knife, and belaying pins could be wielded as improvised clubs. If there were no weapons left the combatants would kick, punch and bite. This was a fight with no holds barred, fought out in a very confined space. The deck on the *Jane* between the main hatch and the bow was just 20ft long, and tapered from 15ft wide amidships to just a single wooden stempost beneath the bowsprit. The deck itself also contained the capstan, a small covered hatch and probably several bodies. The ferocious hand-to-hand fight that followed must have been a brutal and horrific experience.

According to Captain Johnson, 'Blackbeard and the lieutenant fired the first pistol at each other, by which the pirate received a wound'. The two men would have discarded their pistols – probably by throwing them at their opponent – and they then drew their swords. Both men had more than one pistol, but these were single-shot weapons, and it took too long to cock and fire one when your opponent was cutting at you with a sword. Blackbeard was known for his physical strength, as well as for his terrifying appearance and almost psychopathic ferocity. Others would have shied away from him, but Maynard deliberately sought out the pirate captain. This was to be a duel to the death. The *Boston News Letter* described their fight:

> Maynard and Teach themselves begun *[sic]* the fight with their swords, Maynard making a thrust, the point of his sword went against Teach's cartridge box, and bended it to the hilt. Teach broke the guard of it, and wounded Maynard's fingers but did not disable him, whereupon he jumped back and threw away his sword and fired his [second] pistol, which wounded Teach.

This depiction of Blackbeard's last fight was used to illustrate a 19th-century edition of Captain Johnson's account of him. It shows Teach fighting his duel with Maynard, and the crew of the *Jane* emerging from their hiding place in the sloop's hold.

Teach had now been shot twice, but seemed to show no sign of being slowed down. Maynard was now wounded too, and the pirate captain would have closed in for the kill as Maynard discarded his second pistol, and tried to grab another sword from the deck.

While the two captains had been fighting their own private duel the melee swirled around them. The British sailors had a significant advantage over their opponents, as unlike the pirates they had trained for this. Regular cutlass practice, small-arms training and swordsmanship classes had honed them into men that could be relied on in a fight. That meant they had a qualitative edge over the pirates, most of whom came from merchant ships, and rarely practised with their weapons. Gradually the pirates were pushed back towards the *Jane*'s bow, and as men fell the decks became sticky with blood, or sailors stumbled over their dead or wounded companions. This, though, meant that Blackbeard's men who had begun the battle beside him had been pushed back, and the two duellists were now isolated from the main fight.

This also meant that Maynard's men were now able to move behind the pirate captain. For Maynard this meant that he no longer had to fight Blackbeard on his own. Blackbeard knew Maynard was faltering, and raised his cutlass to deliver a killing blow. Then, according to Captain Johnson's version of events, 'one of Maynard's men gave him [Blackbeard] a terrible wound in the neck and throat'. According to the *Boston News Letter* the

This historic marker located in Bath, NC, celebrates the association between the pirate captain and the town. During his stay there Teach rented a house a few miles outside Bath Town, on the southern side of Back Creek, while his men lodged in the town's 'ordinaries' or taverns.

assailant was the British sailor with the Dutch name from New York, Abraham Demelt (or DeMelt). The paper claimed that 'Demelt stuck in between then [them] with his sword, and cut Teach's face pretty much [badly]'. Blackbeard had now been badly wounded, and his face and neck would have been covered in blood, adding to his demonic appearance.

Still he remained standing, swinging his cutlass to keep his two assailants at bay. Now, as the tide of battle turned, other British sailors turned their attention to the pirate captain. Still, as Johnson put it, 'He stood his ground and fought with great fury, 'till he received five and twenty wounds, five of them by shot'. Blackbeard's final moments are recounted in the *Boston News Letter*: 'One of Maynard's men being a Highlander, engaged Teach with his broadsword, who gave Teach a wound in the neck, Teach saying well done lad. The Highlander replied If it be not well done I'll do it better. With that he gave him a second stroke, which cut off his head, laying it flat on his shoulder.'

Captain Johnson's version is much less dramatic, and much more plausible. He recounts how Teach held off all his attackers for a short while – probably less than a minute – as they shot and hacked at him from all sides. Gradually, though, his strength faded from loss of blood, and 'At length, as he was cocking another pistol, having fired several before, he fell down dead'. Maynard merely reported that he had fought Teach and he had been killed, but his lack of detail is typical of after-action service reports from this period. However it happened, Edward Teach, better known as Blackbeard, the most notorious pirate in the Americas, now lay dead at the feet of Lieutenant Maynard.

With their leader gone the fight went out of the remaining pirates. Of the 14 or so pirates who boarded the *Jane*, eight of them had been killed or badly wounded. The remainder either surrendered or jumped overboard, and called out for quarter. During the fight the grappling hooks binding the *Adventure* and the *Jane* together had been severed, probably as the *Jane*'s crew didn't want the remaining pirates to join the fight. They were allowed to surrender and were duly hauled back on board the blood-soaked deck of the *Jane*. There they were kept under guard, and left to patch their wounds as best they could. Both prisoners and captors knew that before long all of these pirates would be facing the gallows.

The whole fight had probably lasted around ten minutes, from the moment the pirates boarded the *Jane* until the last of them surrendered. For those involved, the fighting would have seemed to last an eternity. It was only now that Lieutenant Maynard was able to look about him, and see what was happening beyond the deck of his sloop. The *Adventure* had drifted apart from the *Jane*, so presumably the grappling lines had been cut. While the melee was going on the remainder of the *Ranger*'s crew had refloated their craft, and steered it towards the *Adventure*. There can't have been more than a dozen unwounded men on board the smaller of the two British craft, but when the two ships touched they threw themselves at the ten pirates on board their own sloop. As Captain Johnson put it, 'The sloop *Ranger* came up, and attacked the men that remained in Blackbeard's sloop, with equal bravery, 'till they likewise cried for quarter'.

22 NOVEMBER 1718

9.00am
Teach killed

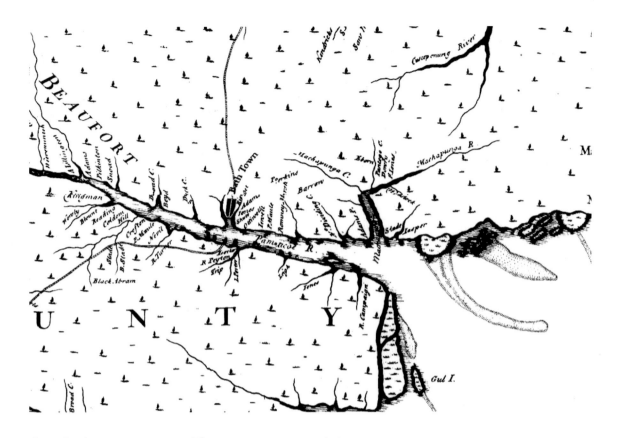

The small settlement of Bath Town is shown on Bath Creek, just above where it flows into the Pamlico River, in this detail of an early 18th-century map of the North Carolina colony. Maynard's original orders were to blockade the river where it enters Pamlico Sound.

The *Jane* now appeared, having covered the intervening few yards to come alongside the unengaged port side of the *Adventure*. The *Ranger* already lay along her port side. The crew of the *Ranger* were busy disarming the pirates, and it was at that moment that a last casualty was suffered by Maynard's force. In his report to the Admiralty, Captain Gordon of the *Lyme* reported that 'taking him by mistake for one of the pirates', a sailor from the *Jane* shot and killed one of the *Ranger*'s crew – a seaman from HMS *Lyme*. Despite this unfortunate accident the pirates were duly taken prisoner, and the British sailors began exploring Blackbeard's sloop, to see if any more of them were hiding below decks.

This was when the last incident of the battle took place. One of Blackbeard's crew was a pirate known as Black Caesar. He was a former slave, and according to Florida legend he and several other West Africans were shipwrecked on the Florida Keys, and took to piracy in order to survive. They used dugout canoes to attack passing ships, and eventually they reached New Providence. There Caesar joined Blackbeard's crew. In his account of the battle Captain Johnson claimed that Blackbeard 'posted a resolute fellow, a Negro, who he had brought up, with a lighted match in the powder room with commands to blow up when he should give him orders'.

Black Caesar stayed below decks during the battle, and when he felt the battle was lost he tried to ignite the powder trail leading to the powder store. Fortunately for everyone on board he was overpowered by the two civilians from the Carolinian trading sloop who had been sleeping off their

Blackbeard's severed head, hanging from the tip of the *Jane*'s bowsprit. This grisly trophy adorned the sloop as it anchored in Bath Creek, when it entered the James River, and when it put in to Jamestown. The skull now forms part of the collection of the Peabody Essex Museum in Salem, MA.

excesses of the night before. They had wisely stayed in the hold when the *Adventure* sailed into battle, and their quick thinking almost certainly averted a disaster. The aftermath of a battle can be a dispiriting time for victors and vanquished alike. Many had seen close friends cut down, others had been wounded, and those who survived were wondering how they escaped with their lives. Maynard ordered the British wounded to be seen to, and had his wounded hand dressed. While this was going on he would have tallied up the cost of the action.

Blackbeard's last fight off Ocracoke, 22 November 1718

On the morning of Friday 22 November Lieutenant Robert Maynard of the Royal Navy led his two small sloops into action against Blackbeard's well-armed vessel, the *Adventure*. As the two forces closed Blackbeard fired a broadside into Maynard's vessels, and the smaller of the two – the *Ranger* – was forced aground on a sandbar. Maynard continued to close with the *Adventure* in his sloop the *Jane*, but Blackbeard decided to board the British vessel before her consort could rejoin the fight. He manoeuvred the *Adventure* so that it came into contact with the *Jane*'s bow, then after lobbing a salvo of grenadoes (grenades) on board Blackbeard and 14 men jumped on board the British craft.

This is the scene depicted here. As Maynard had hidden the larger part of his 35-man crew in the *Jane*'s hold, Blackbeard presumed the defenders were hopelessly outnumbered. Only Maynard and a handful of defenders stood waiting for them on the *Jane*'s deck. As Blackbeard swung aboard, Maynard's men surged up from below decks, and joined in the fight. This tipped the balance in favour of the British sailors, and so Blackbeard found himself fighting for his life. During this period there was little or no difference between the dress of pirates or Royal Naval sailors. Both wore whatever they wanted. It is worth noting that many of the features we now associate with pirate dress, such as headscarves and sashes, were late 19th-century inventions. Instead, the men wore the same garb as other seamen of the period. Maynard was the exception, and he is depicted here in the uniform of an officer of the Royal Navy.

In a letter he wrote three weeks after the battle, Maynard said that on board the *Jane* eight of his men had been killed outright, and 18 more had been wounded. As he only started with 35 men and three civilians under his command this was a high butcher's bill – almost two-thirds of his crew. Maynard's superior claimed that nine men had been killed from the *Pearl* – the men crewing the *Jane* – while two more from the *Lyme* had died – the men from the *Ranger*. The extra fatality may well have been a sailor who succumbed to his wounds, as Brand's report was written after Maynard's letter. Brand added that there were over 20 wounded in both British sloops, while Governor Spotswood later raised the total to 'no less than 12 killed and 22 wounded'. That means that over half of Maynard's force became casualties.

As for the pirates, Blackbeard began the battle with 25 men under his command. By the end of the fighting he and his quartermaster, Thomas Miller, were dead, together with the gunner Philip Morton, the boatswain, the carpenter and four others, a total of nine dead. Captain Gordon of the *Lyme* wrote to the Admiralty saying that 'Teach and five or six of his men were killed', while Spotswood claimed that Blackbeard and nine others were killed, and added that one prisoner subsequently died of his wounds. That left 15 more pirates as prisoners, some of whom were badly wounded. Caring for these enemy wounded would have been a low priority. The sailors earned the same bounty from Governor Spotswood whether their prisoners were brought back dead or alive.

Maynard spent three more days anchored off Ocracoke. He buried his dead at sea, then had the wounded tended, the sloops repaired, and had the blood swabbed off their decks. He sent the trading sloop off to Bath Town with a letter for Captain Brand, outlining what had happened, and his men scoured Ocracoke for any more pirates who had escaped. He found one man hiding in the reeds, betrayed by the ducks hovering overhead. This done, he ordered Blackbeard's head to be hung from the bowsprit of the *Jane*. If the pirate hadn't been decapitated before the battle, it was done now, and the rest of his corpse was unceremoniously dumped over the side. After all, only the head was needed in order to claim the £100 bounty. With this grisly trophy leading the way the three sloops raised anchor, and before setting a course towards Virginia Maynard headed to Bath Town, to report to his superior in person. From there he would return to Virginia, where the prisoners could expect a public trial and execution, and the sailors could look forward to a heroes' welcome.

To Bath Town

While Lieutenant Maynard had been working his way southwards toward Ocracoke, Captain Brand's expedition had been marching south towards Bath Town. It set out for North Carolina on the evening of 17 November, while back in Williamsburg Governor Spotswood was frantically trying to establish a legal case for what was effectively an invasion of a neighbouring state. They marched through what is now Suffolk County, Virginia, skirting the northern and western edges of the extensive marshy area known as the Dismal Swamp. They crossed the boundary into the North Carolina colony somewhere near the present-day town of Whaleyville, Virginia. From there a trail ran southwards.

Before they reached Bath Town they had to cross Albemarle Sound. The sound ran westward from the Outer Banks, before curving northwards to become the Chowan River. If they crossed the river, Brand's men would be faced with another river barring their path – the Roanoke. There the Broadneck Swamp and other marshy wooded ground lined the river for 40 miles, until it finally entered Albemarle Sound. To avoid this would entail a major detour to the west. The Virginian column would then have to find the road running south to Bath Town from the nascent settlement

Although this engraving depicts the execution of 'the gentleman pirate' Stede Bonnet in Charles Town, the scene would have been similar to other pirate executions. The difference in Williamsburg was that the pirates were hanged from trees lining the road to the colony's main port of Jamestown.

near Governor Eden's plantation that in 1722 became Edenton. In 1718 it was known simply as 'the towne on Queen Anne's Creek'. Although it predated Bath Town, this northern settlement was slightly smaller, with less than a dozen buildings, including a half-built courthouse.

Fortunately, Captain Brand had a useful ally. Edward Moseley was an ardent political opponent of Governor Eden, and one of the wealthiest landowners in the North Carolina colony. He was also a lawyer of considerable repute, and an honorary colonel in the colony's militia. He had a house in Bath Town and another in the future Edenton, and it was from this second house that he rode out to meet Captain Brand a few miles to the north, in the northern part of Chowan County. Months before he had written to Governor Spotswood to complain about Eden's association with Teach, and during the ensuing correspondence Moseley offered to help Spotswood rid North Carolina of the pirate. In the process he might be able to oust Eden from the governorship. So, some 10 miles north of Queen Anne's Creek, Moseley and his companion Colonel Moore of the North Carolina militia waited for Brand's column to appear.

This was a crucial development, as Spotswood could argue that he entered North Carolina on the invitation of some of its leading citizens. It also meant that Brand could avoid the swampy Roanoke River, and head straight for Queen Anne's Creek, knowing that Moseley had already

Bath Creek today, viewed from the southern edge of Bath, NC, close to Back Creek. This is where Blackbeard anchored the *Adventure* during his visits to the settlement. Governor Eden's plantation lay a mile inland, beyond the far (western) shore of the creek.

Although Frank Schoonover's depiction of Blackbeard's men entering Charles Town in 1718 is hopelessly inaccurate, it could just as easily depict the entrance of Brand's men into Bath Town several months later.

arranged for ferry boats to transport his force across Pamlico Sound. On 21 November Colonel Brand wrote a letter to the Admiralty, claiming his force was now within 50 miles of Bath Town. This places him in Northern Chowan, where Moseley was waiting for him.

That evening the Virginian column crossed Pamlico Sound, as Colonel Moore's militia guarded the crossing points to prevent word of the invasion reaching Bath Town. The Queen Anne's Creek settlement lay on the north bank of Pamlico Sound, and travellers to Bath Town usually took the ferry to the southern bank, close to where the Albemarle Sound bridge crosses today. This meant that at the very moment when Lieutenant Maynard was fighting his duel with Blackbeard, Captain Brand's column was still 35 miles to the north of Bath Town, at the start of a long day's march.

Of course the original plan was for Maynard to bottle up Blackbeard's adventure in the Pamlico River. If the pirate captain hadn't been at Ocracoke

24 NOVEMBER 1718

Brand's entry into Bath Town

Maynard would have followed his orders, and by the evening of 22 November – the day of the battle – he would have been in place, a few miles downriver from Bath Creek. When Brand appeared two days later the pirates would be caught between the two forces. Without any means of communicating with Maynard, Brand assumed that his march would end in a battle in the streets of Bath Town.

From Pamlico Sound Brand marched south, skirting the western side of two lakes and passing through a landscape of woodland and streams. By 10pm on the evening of Saturday 23 November he was somewhere near the northern end of Bath Creek, and just 3 miles from the town. He inspected his men, checked their weapons, and gave orders for the attack, which would take place the following morning. He had sent Colonel Moore ahead on a reconnaissance, and that evening the North Carolinian reported back, saying that although Teach wasn't in the town, he was expected to arrive there at 'every minute'.

At dawn the following morning Governor Eden was woken up by men banging on his plantation house door. Brand was establishing his legal credentials. He presented Eden with a letter from Spotswood, and informed him he was ordered to hunt down any pirates he encountered. Eden was outraged, but powerless. This was a military *coup de main*, and with his own militia siding with Brand there was little he could do. Eden's plantation was on the west side of Bath Creek. Brand rejoined his main column to the north of Bath Town, and in mid-morning they marched into the small settlement.

In November 1718 Bath Town was little more than a village – a collection of just a few dozen houses, with around 100 non-piratical inhabitants. It lay on the eastern side of the creek, while a second smaller inlet known as Back Creek marked the southern boundary of the settlement. It boasted a mill, a small shipyard, a church and a few taverns, plus several warehouses located along the banks of the creek. Brand marched in from the north, and quickly cordoned off the town. The inhabitants came out to see what was happening, but while they might have been infuriated by this Virginian invasion, they were reassured by the sight of the handful of North Carolina militia and their officers.

What followed was something of an anti-climax. After all this marching there was almost no fighting – at least none that was mentioned in the official reports. No doubt a few pirates tried to escape, or to offer resistance, but they were soon captured or overpowered. Brand had singled out the taverns (known as 'ordinaries') for special attention, as he suspected this was where any pirates would be housed. Six pirates were rounded up, including Blackbeard's first mate Israel Hands. They were duly placed in irons, as Brand stood on the banks of Bath Creek, wondering where Blackbeard could be. After questioning some of the townspeople he learned that the *Adventure* was lying off Ocracoke. Word from Maynard had still not reached him, so that Sunday evening – 24 November – he sent two dugout canoes down the Pamlico River, crewed by his sailors and local guides. Two days later they returned, with news that Blackbeard had been killed, the *Adventure* captured, and the two British sloops were preparing to return to Virginia.

The local trading sloop which had lain next to Blackbeard's vessel off Ocracoke, and which Maynard had despatched after the action, reached Bath Town the following morning – 25 November – and it carried Maynard's brief account of his victory. Brand was delighted. Although his raid hadn't gone exactly according to plan, it had proved a spectacular success. Blackbeard and several of his men had been killed, the rest were about to be shipped back to Virginia to stand trial, and the pirate threat had been crushed. All in all it was a highly satisfactory conclusion to a daring operation.

Naturally Governor Eden didn't share Captain Brand's delight. Over the next few days Brand's men scoured the area for any pirates who might have escaped, and seized goods he believed belonged to Blackbeard. Captain Johnson described the haul as '25 hogsheads of sugar, 11 tierces [barrels] and 145 bags of cocoa, a barrel of indigo, and a bale of cotton'. Most damning of all was the storage of goods taken from the French prizes in Tobias Knight's own barn. While all this didn't sound like much, most of what Blackbeard had plundered from his most recent victims had already been converted into money, and divided among his crew. Most of it had then been squandered in the Bath Town 'ordinaries'. What remained of this personal plunder was no doubt quietly taken by the victors. When the haul was sold, along with the sloop *Adventure*, the total income came to £2,238. This more than paid for the cost of staging the raid, the rewards paid out to the sailors, and the prize money awarded to Brand, Gordon and Maynard.

This, of course, wasn't the end of the story. What followed was one of the most bitter legal wrangles in American colonial history, as Eden, Spotswood and their supporters and detractors argued their cases in court. A bold and daring raid which had been won with cold steel and pistol balls ended in an equally bitter contest, fought out with ink, quill and paper. For the pirates, though, the aftermath of the operation would be altogether more draconian.

The pirate hunters' entry into Bath Town, 1718

On the morning of Sunday 24 November Captain Ellis Brand's column approached Bath Town from the north, on the trail that led northwards to the Queen Anne's Creek settlement. His force of approximately 200 men consisted of British sailors from the frigates HMS *Pearl* and HMS *Lyme*, and a contingent of Virginia militia, supplied by Governor Spotswood of the Virginia colony. The citizens of Bath Town were taken completely by surprise, and while some protested against what amounted to an invasion of the North Carolina colony by neighbouring Virginia, others were assuaged by the presence of King's officers of the Royal Navy, and by officers of the North Carolina militia, led by Colonel Edward Moseley.

In this scene Captain Brand can be seen dressed in the full-dress coat of a post captain in the Royal Navy, while his men wear the non-uniform garb of British sailors of the period, augmented by warm clothing and their weapons – an assortment of muskets, pistols and cutlasses drawn from the ships' stores. Brand is accompanied by officers of the Virginia and North Carolina militias – both wore the same red-coated uniform, but like the sailors the militiamen themselves weren't issued with a uniform during this period. The townspeople of Bath Town are dressed in their typical Sunday garb, and watch or offer protest as the column enters their town, and begins rounding up anyone suspected of being a pirate. During this operation six pirates were arrested in Bath Town, including Blackbeard's first mate Israel Hands.

AFTERMATH AND ANALYSIS

Trial and punishment

The whole operation had been carried out for one specific purpose. Governor Spotswood wanted to send a clear message to other would-be pirates that he and others like him were no longer prepared to offer pardons or forgive crimes. They were determined to drive pirates from American waters, and wanted the death of Blackbeard to signal that the days of these pirates were numbered. In fact the attack was only the first half of this exercise in statement-making. The second part revolved around the very public trial and execution of Blackbeard's crew.

The captured pirates were gathered in Bath Town, and the majority of them then marched north under armed guard, accompanied by the men of Captain Brand's column, and several wagon-loads of plunder. They left at the start of December, but bad weather delayed their progress. It was 18 December when they arrived in Williamsburg, and the pirates were finally incarcerated in the town gaol. Three days later Brand and his men returned to the *Pearl*.

A few days before the pirates started their long walk into captivity, Maynard had put to sea in his two sloops, and set a course for the James River. On 1 December the crew of the *Pearl* and the *Lyme* saw the *Jane* and *Ranger* approaching with their prize, with Blackbeard's head still swinging from the *Jane*'s bowsprit. The sailors lined the decks to give Maynard and his men the heroes' welcome they deserved. Maynard's men cheered back.

After reporting to Captain Gordon, Maynard offloaded his own wounded, then continued on to Jamestown, carrying the pirates who were too badly wounded to make the journey on foot. They too were eventually deposited in the Williamsburg gaol. Similarly, many townspeople would have made

The execution of pirates was a public affair, attended by a large crowd, eager to watch the miscreant's final moments. This was encouraged by the authorities, as it served to spread the message that there would be no clemency for convicted pirates.

the 8-mile journey to Jamestown, to welcome their naval heroes. More than a few also wanted to catch a glimpse of Blackbeard's severed head.

As for his crew, they languished in prison for three months. There were 16 of them, including the unfortunate Samuel Odel, one of the two Carolina traders who were caught on board the pirate sloop when she was captured. Five pirates had secretly offered to testify against their fellow pirates in order to escape the gallows; four of these turncoats were former slaves, and the fifth was Blackbeard's first mate, Israel Hands. His testimony would help to hang many of his former shipmates.

The trial began on 12 March 1719, and was held in the Capitol building in Williamsburg. The trial was conducted under Admiralty law, which

meant that there wasn't a jury. Spotswood presided, supported by the leading judiciaries in the colony. The charges were read out, and evidence was supplied that Blackbeard and the men on trial had continued their attacks after receiving their pardon. This of course was the crux of the case against them.

There was little chance of any leniency. For Spotswood the main aim of the trial was to discredit Governor Eden. By proving the pirates had seized the two French ships illegally he would expose Eden's award of salvage rights to Teach as little more than a cover-up. The damning letter written by Tobias Knight merely added to the sense of a conspiracy between the pirates and the North Carolinian authorities. The Vice-Admiralty court came to a speedy verdict. All but one of the condemned men was found guilty of piracy and sentenced to death. This included all of the former slaves who had given testimony. The one prisoner who escaped the ultimate sentence was Samuel Odel, the sailor from Bath Town. He was set free with a warning about the dangers of falling into bad company.

The mass execution of the pirates took place a few days later, along the road leading into Jamestown. One after the other they were placed, standing, on the back of a cart, a noose was thrown over a tree at the side of the road, and the cart was wheeled away, leaving the condemned man hanging. One pirate escaped execution that day. At the last minute Israel Hands received a pardon. It was given because Blackbeard had shot him in the knee during an altercation, and so he was recovering in Bath Town when Blackbeard attacked the two French ships. Technically he was still covered by the pardon. In reality the last-minute pardon was a reward for turning informant.

The legal wrangling rumbled on for years, lasting until Governor Eden's death in 1722. The first round was fought out in North Carolina itself. Edward Moseley accused Eden of profiting from piracy, but was arrested on the governor's orders. In a trial orchestrated by Eden, Moseley was duly found guilty of 'issuing seditious words', fined, and barred from holding public office. He resumed his public duties after Eden's death. Eden himself was cleared of any charges of wrongdoing by the colony's Provincial Council, which as far as he was concerned was the end of the matter.

Alexander Spotswood had other plans. First he attacked Tobias Knight, accusing him of colluding with Blackbeard. Evidence included the testimony of the captured pirates, the letter found on board the *Adventure*, and the plunder found in Knight's barn. In May 1719 he was brought to trial in a Vice-Admiralty court, but this was held in North Carolina, not Virginia, and Governor Eden presided. Hardly surprisingly, Knight was found not guilty. Knight died shortly afterwards, after suffering from a lingering illness which some unkindly said was brought about by guilt. As a result Spotswood's case against Eden collapsed, and despite virulent protests to London no further enquiry into the affair was convened before Eden's death. For his part Eden waged his own legal campaign, accusing Spotswood and Brand of a whole range of crimes, none of which was valid. The matter degenerated into a regular flurry of legal missives, which benefited nobody but the lawyers.

Spotswood was much less effective when it came to paying the pirate hunters. Maynard and his men were due a bounty of around £1,200 between them, but it took the Virginian clerks more than four years to pay what they owed. Even then they got it wrong – the reward was divided among the entire crew of the *Pearl* and the *Lyme*, including those who had taken no part in the expedition. That meant those who risked their lives in battle with Blackbeard only received a fraction of what they had been promised.

As for Maynard, he got into trouble for distributing the few coins and other trinkets found on the *Adventure* between his surviving crew. It was divided between the 47 survivors of the battle – the only reward for their services that many of these men ever received. When HMS *Pearl* returned to Britain in 1721 Maynard resigned his commission, and rejoined his family in Kent. However, he later rejoined the service, and ended his career with the rank of master and commander. He died in Great Mongeham in Kent in 1751, aged 67.

His superior Captain Brand shrugged off the writs issued by Governor Eden, and reached flag rank in the War of Jenkins' Ear (1739–48). Governor Spotswood survived the political fallout of the pirate-hunting raid, but he fell foul of his more domestic political opponents and was replaced as governor in 1722. He went back to London, where he married, but returned to

The North Carolina Maritime Museum in Beaufort, NC, contains a large number of artefacts recovered from the *Queen Anne's Revenge*, which foundered just a few miles away from where the museum now stands. This display contains ordnance-related items recovered from Blackbeard's 40-gun flagship.

After being executed, pirates' bodies were often coated in tar to preserve them, and were then displayed in iron cages sited at the entrance to a harbour, to serve as a warning to others. Legend has it Blackbeard's head was displayed in this manner at Newport News, Virginia.

Virginia shortly afterwards, and died in Maryland in 1740. Although Spotswood fell victim to political intrigue, the two men who carried out his raid both prospered in the years following the operation. This is hardly surprising, as its planning and execution demonstrated an impressive ability for leadership and motivation, as well as courage.

Analysis

All four of the organizers – Governor Spotswood, Captains Brand and Gordon and Lieutenant Maynard – had each contributed something to ensure the success of the operation. Spotswood had used his political abilities to undermine Governor Eden's legal case, and to ensure the vital co-operation of Edward Moseley. Without his help Brand would have been hard-pressed to reach Bath Town without the pirates learning of his approach. His offer of a reward also helped to motivate the seamen, and ensured they had something worth fighting for apart from the honour of the service.

George Gordon provided the logistical support for the operation, and supervised the preparation of Maynard's naval force. The provision of local pilots was a crucial factor in ensuring Maynard's success, and his decision to leave the two sloops unarmed – he could easily have provided guns for them – was a difficult one to make. However, on the advice of the pilots it was decided that these would increase the displacement of the two sloops, and so make them less effective in the shallow waters of Pamlico Sound.

Ellis Brand was the man who first conceived this two-pronged attack, as he saw it as the only way to prevent the pirates from slipping through his net. His decision to use local sloops for the naval attack was largely due to their availability, but he could have carried out the assault another way, by sailing the two frigates to the mouth of Ocracoke Inlet, and then sending a cutting-out expedition in to attack Blackbeard's ship. That was a sensible enough plan if Teach was at Ocracoke, but the intelligence reports Brand had at his disposal suggested the *Adventure* was 50 miles away to the west, in Bath Creek. That was too far for his men to travel comfortably in ship's boats, so the sloops were really the only viable option available to him. Besides, by using local craft the pirates might question their identity long enough for Maynard to close the range.

During the land operation Brand took command of his joint force of Virginia militia and sailors, and drove them hard. The result was a fast advance across North Carolina: this speed reduced the possibility of word reaching the pirates, and of the local population offering resistance. To reduce this risk still further his co-operation with the North Carolina militiamen loyal to Edward Moseley was crucial in allaying the fears of the Carolinians, and preventing word of the column's approach reaching Bath Town.

Then there was Robert Maynard. His cool leadership under fire proved crucial on that cold November morning. First of all, while he expected to encounter Blackbeard a day's sail away across Pamlico Sound, his quick thinking allowed him to launch a well-conceived and thoroughly well-executed attack off Ocracoke, when the *Adventure* was sighted lying off the island. His decision to wait until dawn was crucial, too, as it gave his sober crewmen a slight edge over their adversaries. His decision to hide a large portion of his crew below decks proved critical when the boarding action started.

He realized that Teach had guns on his sloop, so it was imperative to close the distance as quickly as possible – hence the use of sails and sweeps. When the two sides came into contact with each other it was unfortunate that the *Ranger* was temporarily put out of action, but Maynard didn't hesitate in closing with the enemy. Whatever the odds, he knew that boldness was the key to victory against these pirates. Then, when the fighting started he displayed his courage by singling out Blackbeard – a fearsome opponent – as he realized that without their leader, the pirates' morale would crumble.

The raid can be held up as a perfect example of an anti-piracy operation. The combination of a land attack and a seaborne one was repeated in later similar anti-piracy missions carried out by the Royal Navy in West Africa and the Persian Gulf during the age of sail, and by the US Navy in the Caribbean. It was a bold plan, and it worked to perfection. This though, was largely down to the raw courage of a handful of British sailors, and the audacity of a plucky middle-aged lieutenant.

CONCLUSION

The events of November 1718 formed a pivotal part in the war against piracy. Governor Spotswood's message had been clear and unequivocal. Piracy didn't pay. The pirate scourge would continue for several more years, but this attack, together with the establishment of British rule in the Bahamas, effectively marked the beginning of the end for piracy in the Americas. In the Bahamas Governor Rogers hanged any pirates who were caught after returning to their old ways, as a warning to the others.

One other event underlined the point. After being abandoned by Teach, Stede Bonnet headed south, and found a temporary refuge in the Cape Fear River. It was there that he was discovered and captured by two pirate-hunting sloops sent out from Charles Town. Ironically, they were looking for Blackbeard, but the unfortunate Bonnet was caught instead. He and his men were tried in Charles Town, and in December 1718 they were hanged. The mass pirate executions in Charles Town, Williamsburg and New Providence all played an important part in discouraging other former pirates from recrossing the line.

This all formed part of a wider strategy. While Blackbeard's blockade of Charles Town had caused a sensation in colonial America, it was merely the most daring of a number of pirate attacks that were undermining maritime trade, from Newfoundland to Brazil, off the West African coast, and in the Indian Ocean. The 'carrot and stick' policy of George I's government was effective, but in 1718 there was little sign that the policy was working, as those pirates who refused the pardon or who reverted to piracy continued the depredations. The closing of the Bahamas to them merely drove some of them elsewhere, to new hunting grounds off the slave coasts of West Africa, or the waters off Madagascar.

The operation against Blackbeard marked the start of the 'stick'. In the years that followed the other notorious pirates of the age would be cornered, captured and either killed or executed – men like 'Black Sam' Bellamy, 'Calico Jack' Rackam, Charles Vane, George Lowther, and 'Black Bart' Roberts.

By 1722 the worst had passed, and while a few pirates remained at large, the great scourge was effectively over.

Two years later, in May 1724, Captain Charles Johnson published his *General History of Pyrates*, a book that became an instant bestseller. It remains in print today. Some argue that Johnson was a *nom de plume* for Daniel Defoe, but unfortunately the author's identity remains a mystery. However, his retelling of the tale of Blackbeard was the first stage in the process that turned a man who was merely a dangerous and notorious criminal into one of the most easily recognized pirates in history. As a result, Blackbeard became a figure of legend – a myth more than a man. This book is an attempt to uncover the real Blackbeard, and to unravel the events surrounding his death, in what was probably the most dramatic anti-piracy raid of 'The Golden Age of Piracy'.

Archaeologists recovering a concretion-encrusted gun – a cast-iron 6-pounder – from the wreck of Blackbeard's flagship *Queen Anne's Revenge*. After extensive conservation the weapon formed part of the collection of the North Carolina Maritime Museum.

BIBLIOGRAPHY

Albury, Paul, *The Story of the Bahamas*, London (1975)

Baer, Joel, *Pirates of the British Isles*, Stroud (2005)

Blackmore, Howard L., *Armouries of the Tower of London: Catalogue: Volume 1: Ordnance*, London (1977)

Bradlee, Francis B.C., Piracy *in the West Indies and its Suppression*, Glorietta, NM (1990)

Brock, R.A. (ed.), *Official Letters of Alexander Spotswood*, Richmond, VA (1885)

Burgess, Robert F. & Clausen, Carl J., *Florida's Golden Galleons: The Search for the 1715 Treasure Fleet*, Port Salerno, FL (1982)

Cordingly, David, *Under the Black Flag: The Romance and the Reality of Life among the Pirates*, London (1995)

Dabney, Virginius, *Virginia: The New Dominion*, Charlottesville, VA (1983)

Davis, Ralph, *The Rise of the Atlantic Economies*, London (1973)

Dodson, Leonidas, *Alexander Spotswood: Governor of Colonial Virginia*, Philadelphia, PA (1932)

Earle, Peter, *The Pirate Wars*, London (2003)

Fraser, Walter J., *Charleston! Charleston!: The History of a Southern City*, Columbia, SC (1992)

Gosse, Philip, *The Pirate's Who's Who*, Glorietta, NM (1988)

Havighurst, Walter, *Alexander Spotswood: A Portrait of a Governor*, New York, NY (1967)

Johnson, Captain Charles, *A General History of the Robberies & Murders of the Most Notorious Pirates* (ed. David Cordingly), London (1998)

Johnson, Paul, *A History of the American People*, New York, NY (1997)

Jones, Hugh, *The Present State of Virginia*, Richmond, VA (1912)

Konstam, Angus, *The History of Pirates*, New York, NY (1999)

Konstam, Angus, *Blackbeard: America's Most Notorious Pirate*, Hoboken, NJ (2006)

Konstam, Angus, *Piracy: The Complete History*, Oxford (2008)

Lee, Robert E., *Blackbeard the Pirate: A Reappraisal of his Life and Times*, Winston-Salem, NC (1974)

Little, Benerson, *A Sea Rover's Practice: Pirate Tactics and Techniques, 1630–1730*, Dulles, VA (2005)

Lyon, David, *The Sailing Navy List: All of the Ships of the Royal Navy, Built, Purchased and Captured, 1688–1860*, London (2001)

McIlwaine, H.R. (ed.), *Executive Journals, Council of Virginia*, Richmond, VA (1928)

Marx, Jennifer, *Pirates and Privateers of the Caribbean*, Malabar, FL (1992)

Parry, Dan, *Blackbeard: The Real Pirate of the Caribbean*, London (2006)

Paschal, Herbert L., A *History of Colonial Bath*, Raleigh, NC (1955)

Rankin, Hugh F., *The Pirates of Colonial North Carolina*, Raleigh, NC (1981)

Rediker, Marcus, *Between the Devil and the Deep Blue Sea: Merchant Seamen, Pirates and the Anglo-American Maritime World, 1700–1750*, Cambridge (1987)

Rediker, Marcus, *Villains of all Nations: Atlantic Pirates in the Golden Age*, Boston, MA (2004)

Roberts, Nancy, *Blackbeard and other Pirates of the Atlantic Coast*, Winston-Salem, NC (1995)

Rogoziński, Jan, *Honour among Thieves*, London (2000)

Rosen, Robert N., *A Short History of Charleston*, Columbia, SC (1992)

Starkey, David, Van Eyk, E.S. & De Moor, J.A., *Pirates and Privateers: New Perspectives on the War on Trade in the Eighteenth and Nineteenth Centuries*, Exeter (1997)

Tindall, George B. & Shi, David E., *America: A Narrative History*, New York, NY (1989)

Winston, Alexander, *No Purchase, No Pay: Sir Henry Morgan, Captain William Kidd, Captain Woodes Rogers in the Great Age of Privateers and Pirates, 1665–1715*, London (1970)

Woodbury, George, *The Great Days of Piracy in the West Indies*, New York, NY (1951)

Another depiction of Blackbeard wearing the fur hat commonly sported by sailors during winter, and produced for an early edition of Captain Johnson's *General History*. Given that the pirate is holding a scimitar rather than a cutlass, the accuracy of this engraving is questionable.

INDEX

References to illustrations and plates are shown in **bold**. Captions to plates are shown in brackets.